Great Scot

*The Life Story
of Sir Harry Lauder,
Legendary Laird of the Music Hall*

Gordon Irving

LESLIE FREWIN : LONDON

First Published 1968 by Leslie Frewin Publishers Limited,
15 Hay's Mews, Berkeley Square, London W1

This book is set in Bembo
Printed by Anchor Press and
bound by William Brendon,
both of Tiptree, Essex

World Rights Reserved

09 089070 1

Contents

Introduction

WALKING DOWN BROADWAY on a stifling midsummer day in June, I looked up at the surrounding New York skyscrapers and saw the temperature reading on a rooftop. In bold figures the flickering sign announced to the teeming, steaming world below that it was 101 degrees.

I wore a typically British suit, well-tailored and warm. I sweltered – and took off my jacket to carry it over my arm.

At that very moment a stocky little figure appeared in front, walking jauntily towards me. He was a visitor to New York, a man from Canada – and he wore a Balmoral bonnet and a kilt.

There wasn't a cooler person on Broadway on that scorching June midday. The Scottish kilt was proving one of its least-sung virtues – its extreme coolness in the hottest weather.

But that little fellow in the kilt also proved something else, something much more significant and interesting. It was a moment to remember.

As he swung past me, kilt proudly swinging, and dozens of New York heads a-turning, a New York cab-driver slowed down, hung out from his window, and hollered: 'Gee, if it ain't Sir Harry Lauder himself . . . !'

There, in the late 'sixties of the twentieth century, spoke up an American who had, somehow, seized all the implications of the Scottish kilt and was linking it with one man, an artiste and entertainer born nearly one hundred years before, in 1870.

A sturdy little man in a kilt and Balmoral. That's the picture nearly every American keeps in his mind's-eye of the great Sir Harry Lauder, a Scot whose songs still go ringing merrily round the globe in an age of pop and 'beat' and millions of shrieking transistors.

There are many stories told about Harry Lauder. In his lifetime he became a legend. After his death they are still talking about him. He did more than any other person to propagate the image of the Scot.

Internationally, he became the best-known Scotsman of all time. Of that there is no doubt. He has beaten to the publicity post dozens of other great Scots – from William Wallace and Robert the Bruce to Bonnie Prince Charlie and Sir Walter Scott. I'd dare to say, too, that he gained more world-wide spotlighting during his lifetime than even the poet Robert Burns, whom he so much admired.

Walk down any street today in New York or Chicago, Los Angeles or Melbourne, Toronto or Cape Town or Singapore – if ever you chance upon a little man in a Scottish kilt, as well you may, the immediate image to most of the folk around you will be a remembrance of – yes, Sir Harry Lauder.

You can hear his gags and lilting tunes, his songs about lassies and lochs, wives and weans, on any radio station anywhere in the world. It has been rightly estimated that a Sir Harry Lauder melody is being played somewhere, by someone, every hour of every day in every year.

But it wasn't the endearing popularity of Lauder the music-hall star, or the universal character of Lauder the man, that prompted me to start this biography of him.

Many years of meeting and talking with stage stars, of listening to their big-talk and small-talk, and of sympathising, often so objectively, with their many hopes and fears, have inspired me to probe behind the Harry Lauder legend, and to find the secret of it all – how, in fact, a simple-living Scotsman from the Lanarkshire coal-pits, in the heart of Scotland, could rise from extreme poverty to become the greatest comedy-singer and music-hall philosopher of all time. The story of Lauder was calling out to be written following his death midway through the twentieth century.

Oh, yes, Harry Lauder had his faults, like all great stars and men. He was no shining superman in a kilt. I don't set out to overload this wonderful story with eulogy upon eulogy, or to sentimentalise with false praise. He was as human as anybody.

Remove the aura of a music-hall star, and you have an ordinary man with ordinary feelings, fears and doubts. But how he made use of his talents!

Harry Lauder had an over-riding simplicity of style and appeal that has survived his death, and now makes him shine even more strongly and brightly in an allegedly smart and sophisticated age. The wee man with the homely philosophy was as smart as any of your modern wit-and-skit types. And a hundred times more genuine.

He believed sincerely in every word he sang. These words, too, were intelligible and clear. There was nothing vague and non-sensical in the lines of his lyrics. His songs had a lasting quality, thanks to their inherent simplicity.

His humour, too, punctuated with gems of homespun philosophy, was clear and clean and bright. There were no 'sick' jokes among those he spun. Rather, by their utter simplicity, some may appear slightly naive and even 'corny' today. They don't all have that subtle twist expected by a modern generation; in fact, few of them do.

During his lifetime Harry Lauder put pen to paper himself to recount many of his adventures, notably in his book, *Roamin' In The Gloamin'*. But they are concerned with only the earlier part of his life and career.

This biography is the result of the assembling of many anecdotes and facts about the great international minstrel. It is also the result of a personal acquaintance with Sir Harry and his family, especially in his latter years and in the eventide of his life when he had time and leisure to talk and reminisce and laugh over incidents in an unusually busy and picturesque life in Scotland and a wide variety of countries across the seas.

The task of probing behind the Great Scot and his legendary fame has been a most pleasant and exciting one. In the course of it I have unearthed, I trust, not a few new slants on Lauder and his career, and I have been eager to look at him not purely from a Scottish eye, but as he appeared to overseas showbusiness personalities like Eddie Cantor, Charlie Chaplin, Danny Kaye, Max Gordon (the New York writer and producer), and many others.

I believe that any book on Harry Lauder must take a world viewpoint, just as Lauder himself was so clever to do both as a music-hall artiste and as a Scotsman.

Half a century before the general mass of today's entertainers started to travel, Harry Lauder was pioneering in that direction. And this in days when air, sea and land transportation was not nearly so highly developed as it is in today's jet age.

Today it is quite the thing – in fact, sometimes a necessity! – for any leading star to keep travelling. Television can exhaust so much material so quickly. Top artistes can interchange between New York and London, Los Angeles and Cape Town, Montreal and Melbourne and Glasgow, with the greatest of ease.

Harry Lauder did just that, but not, mark you, because he had to. He travelled thousands of miles because his public demanded to see him – in the flesh. His fame preceded him by word of mouth, and curious Americans and Australians and New Zealanders wanted to prove that such a comical and entertaining Great Scot really did exist.

I have been helped in the writing of this book by many people, not least the theatrical folk of Bonnie Scotland who knew Lauder intimately and have never praised him as much as their American friends.

Abel Green, editor of *Variety* of New York, has proved a fountain of knowledge and international showbusiness contacts.

A keen student of international theatre who lives in South Portland, Maine, USA, Mr Harlan F Bradford, has also weighed-in with dates and statistics from the remarkable card-index file he keeps of world vaudeville artistes. His system is so excellent that he has been able to pinpoint for me exactly what acts were on the bill in support of Harry Lauder at the Shubert Theatre in Boston, Massachusetts, in that first week of January 1913 when the Great Scot went over so big with audiences.

The British Music-hall Society, with its headquarters in London, is a valued organisation which has also been of considerable aid in my researches. Mr Ellis Ashton, its publicity officer, has proved most co-operative in delving into its records and playbills, and in providing some of the rare old photographs of Harry Lauder which are contained in these pages.

I am also indebted to Mr Alastair M Dunnett, editor of *The Scotsman*, Edinburgh, who has loaned some very interesting and rarely-seen photographs of various stages in Harry Lauder's career from the art-department files of that newspaper.

Dozens of others, too numerous to mention specifically, have also proved of immense help in the writing of this romantic story of rags to riches, of a penniless Scots laddie who overcame so many difficulties to rise to the top of his chosen profession and become an honoured guest in high places from Buckingham Palace and Balmoral Castle to the White House in Washington, DC.

11

It is a warm and human story that brings in many of the great ones of the world over a period of eight decades. It is a story that has needed no embellishments to keep it interesting. Harry Lauder and his wonderfully varied adventures have seen to that.

G I

The Boy Harry

MANY GREAT MEN start from small beginnings. Maybe you've noticed that the famous and the rich in this world are often those who come from the humblest homes and with the poorest of backgrounds.

Harry Lauder fits right into this pattern. He was a poor Scots laddie born in a tiny home in the seaside town of Portobello, a few miles from Edinburgh, on the 4th August 1870. His early boyhood was spent in the humble family home at Number Three Bridge Street in Portobello. It was a simple, cottage-like birthplace, not far removed from the same modest style of home that had seen the early days of another great Scot, the poet Robert Burns.

The Lauder family didn't have many of the good things of life. Harry's father, John Lauder, was a simple potter. Diligently, he helped to turn out bottles for lemonade and jam. He worked hard in a little pottery in the district.

John Lauder's ancestors were some of the fighting men of the Borderland of Scotland, land of hills and rivers and moors to the south of Portobello and Edinburgh. Harry's grandfather hailed from the district of Lauderdale, in Berwickshire, close to the English. He, too, was known as John Lauder, and he worked as a carpenter.

Grandfather Lauder used to boast that he was really a 'Lauder of the Bass'. This was a reference to the Bass Rock, a rocky islet in the Firth of Forth, which John Lauder claimed had once been the base for a group of nasty Scottish pirates.

On his mother's side Harry had links with the Scottish Highlands. She was a MacLennan, christened Isabella Urquhart MacLeod MacLennan, and her ancestors had come from the Black Isle, that lovely part of Scotland in Ross-shire, just north of Inverness, the Highland capital.

What could be a better background than this for any true Scotsman, a wee bit of both the Highlands and the Lowlands in his blood! Harry was to be proud of both.

As with so many boys who later become great men, Harry was much influenced by his mother. She was a dyed-in-the-tartan Highlander, and the love of the Highland hills and lochs was to be shown later in the songs her son wrote and sang and made famous. Isabella MacLennan Lauder used to regale the whole family in that little Portobello home with romantic tales of Highland witches, fairies and folklore.

So it was that the grandeur of mountain and glen, loch and river came to young Lauder in his most impressionable boyhood years. Mother Lauder would tell the family long and compelling stories of the Highland clans and their adventures o'er moorland and mountain.

Harry was the eldest in a family of eight. Next to him came Matthew, then George, Jock, Alick, Bella, Mary and Jean. As the eldest, Harry had great responsibilities, and he was to shoulder them, of necessity, from his earliest years.

The Lauder home in Bridge Street was small. It was also poor. John Lauder, not always in the best of health, didn't earn a large wage. There were many mouths to feed. Britain had no useful family allowances in 1870.

So Harry Lauder, eldest of the family, was put out early to earn money to augment the family income. One of his first jobs was to help a local Portobello man with the feeding of his pigs. Another

14

was to work for a market gardener, helping to pick his strawberries.

The boy Lauder came to appreciate money thus early. He was happy, some days, when his earnings totalled the princely sum of – fourpence! But there were extra pennies to be picked up as a boy caddie to the rich golfers who came down from Edinburgh in their carriages to golf on the Musselburgh links, within sight of the Firth of Forth.

As the wealthy golfers arrived, wee Harry would push forward with the other lads, crying: 'Carry your clubs, sir?'

The pay for caddies wasn't too bad. Usually, it amounted to twopence a round. Sometimes there was even an extra penny at the end of a round – that is, if you did your work well and lost no balls.

A Scots laddie didn't do too badly at the golf caddie-ing. Top money could be earned if you worked hard. Some days there was as much as ninepence to be earned by dusk; on those days Harry considered himself a millionaire.

Wee Harry counted his pennies and ran home, proud to hand his mother the takings, small though they may appear by comparison with today's rates for the job.

He was a willing laddie, happy and ready to run errands for his mother or to help bath the other children in the large family.

At night, before the family went to sleep, Mrs Lauder would entertain the five boys and three girls with stories from the past. There were wild tales from the Highlands and romantic stories about great Scottish heroes like Robert the Bruce or William Wallace, David Livingstone the explorer or Robert Burns the poet. Young Harry, his brothers and sisters, were to hear much about Bonnie Scotland, its towns and glens and cities. For Isabella MacLennan Lauder had herself a great love for her native land, and particularly the Highlands.

No wonder all these grand fireside tales gave Harry what he described, in later life, as 'a devouring passion for my native land'.

Schooldays were, if not the happiest, certainly the most impressionable days of young Lauder's life. Harry started classes when he was five, and the memory of that first classroom never left him. It became so indelibly imprinted on his mind that, in later years, he was to keep a scale wooden model of his classroom (both that at Portobello and the one at Arbroath) in the Lauder museum room, and show it off proudly to visitors.

The school was a tiny one, not far from the pottery where Harry's father worked. The teacher was memorable, too, a man who, like so many early Scottish teachers or dominies, instilled much fear into the boys in his charge. He was a bearded Scot who gave his young pupils all the basics of the three Rs of early Scottish education – reading, 'riting and 'rithmetic.

The good folk of Portobello and Musselburgh were simple, homely and humble types, not asking for much and making the most of so little. Many were fisherfolk. Lots of the women went round as fishwives, selling the produce of the sea their menfolk had brought home. All had humble but neat little homes. Life was always hard and always earnest. But there was so much work to do nobody had time to ponder and become discontented.

In later life many people asked Harry Lauder why he had not been christened John, like his grandfather and father before him.

Harry himself never quite worked that one out, but he had the impression, somehow, that his father had not been on the best of terms with his grandfather when he was born. The father and son appeared to have had a tiff or something. So it was decided, when the first-born arrived, that he should be called after his mother's father, Henry MacLennan.

Because of that simple enough quarrel, the world missed

knowing a Scottish comedian who might have been named plain Jock Lauder!

Young Harry had happy memories of his maternal grandfather, for old Henry MacLennan, from the Black Isle, had come down from the Highlands to live with his daughter and son-in-law at their Portobello home, in south-east Scotland. Old Henry spoke the Gaelic, the ancient tongue of Scotland, and he used to instil good living into his wee grandson with instructions like: 'Ach, Harry lad, you must be a goot poy an' aye fear the Lord.'

Life was hard and earnest for the Lauders of Portobello in the 'seventies and early 'eighties of last century. Soon they moved home to nearby Musselburgh, so that the whole family could be closer to the pottery where John Lauder worked.

All week the good folk of the seaside town slogged and slaved at their jobs. But, come Sunday, it was, without a doubt, the Sabbath day, and strict rules were observed. The blinds in the little houses were drawn, good books were read, and the little ones trooped to Sunday school and church. Isabella and John Lauder told the family stirring and heroic stories of history and religion, and long passages were read from the Bible.

Harry's father didn't earn much money, but he was a good potter. His main interest, outside of his family, was the sport of running and foot-racing. He trained many of the older lads in the district for the mile and long-distance runs, and one year had the good fortune to train the winner of the famous Powderhall Handicap, a classic race in Scotland.

When Harry Lauder reached his twelfth birthday, he came home from school one day to hear dramatic news.

His father had been offered a much better job and a fatter wage-packet, but far away to the south in England – at Whittington Moor, in Derbyshire. The family would have to pull up their Scottish roots and head for – yes, England.

No more adventures by the shores of the Forth for Harry, his brothers and sisters! No more caddie-ing on the Musselburgh links! No more jaunts on holidays into the big and dignified capital city of Edinburgh where the rich gentry lived in their fine big houses.

A man had no option but to go where the best work was offered, and Isabella MacLennan Lauder and her little brood knew there was no alternative. The family packed up their humble belongings, and left for the south, England – and tragedy.

Through the Mill

So THE POOR and humble family of Lauders – John, the hard-working head of the household, Isabella the mother, and the eight little children – took the road south from Scotland into England.

It was not a journey any of them relished very much. The youngsters had grown accustomed to life in and around Mussel-burgh, by the bracing shores of the Firth of Forth, and had many friends among the neighbours in the trim, well-kept homes close to their own.

Despite the hard chores of helping with the house and looking after his brothers and sisters, young Harry enjoyed the life. Because he enjoyed being a Scot, the move to England did not particularly appeal.

His mother, too, had some foreboding about the transfer south. She wasn't keen on it, and her heart was at home in Bonnie Scotland, among her ain folk. But she said nothing at the time; the move was much too important for her husband John, who saw a better and brighter future for the whole family in the fuller wage-packet he was being offered.

After three weeks spent in packing up their modest belongings and saying goodbye to friends and neighbours, the Lauder family were on their way over the Border – and to unexpected events that were to alter the whole course of life for them once more.

John Lauder found that the job offered him in Pearson's Pottery, at Whittington Moor, in Derbyshire, was a good one, and he prepared to settle in. The nearest large town was Chesterfield, and the Scots family Lauder from north of the Tweed looked wide-eyed in wonder at the new and busy life of the English Midlands.

Their broad, lilting East Scotland accents didn't prove too clear to their new English neighbours, and the way of living was different. But it was at least interesting. As it transpired, they were to have only a few weeks in which to sample the new life and the unfamiliar area of the Potteries countryside.

John Lauder, never the strongest of men, caught a chill, and was sent to bed. The chill turned, unfortunately, to pneumonia, and nothing in the doctor's skill could save him. He grew weaker as the days and nights passed. Harry's mother sensed that the worst was to come, and she leaned more than ever on her eldest son.

It was the year 1882, and Harry Lauder never forgot the drama of that moment as his father lay dying, a comparatively young man of thirty-one, or the sobbing mother who came running from his little bedroom to tell the anxious and distraught family: 'Oh, Harry, Harry, yer faither's deid. The puir man's been taken from us.'

The little family was stranded amid strangers in a distant country, and they thought immediately of their friends and relations up north in Scotland.

There was really nothing young Harry could do but comfort his mother as best a lad could, and get on with the job of helping with the funeral arrangements. But it was a household of deep and genuine mourning at Whittington Moor on that sad day of death in the winter of 1882.

Canny like so many Scots, John Lauder had insured himself for fifteen pounds. It was a considerable sum for those days, and the money, fortunately, was sufficient to give him a decent burial in the little churchyard at Whittington, and to leave a small sum over.

The managers at the pottery were also helpful. They threw in some extra money, and that sum, added to what was left over from the insurance pay-out, proved just enough to take the Lauder family back north to Scotland and their friends. Relatives of Harry's mother lived in the east of Scotland fishing town of Arbroath, and they had indicated they would take the stranded family in and help them. The change of scene was refreshing, and the Lauders faced up to the future again.

Harry, now twelve years old, was fascinated by the new surroundings in the busy east coast town with its population of some twenty thousand, and often wandered down to the little harbour to see the cargo ships come in, ready to disgorge their cargoes of raw flax from Russia and the Baltic lands. This was a new world; it fired his enthusiasm for sailors and ships and little-known foreign countries across the seas. But he had a mother and seven brothers and sisters to maintain. There was work to do. He walked into Gordon's Mill, a local flax-works, and asked for a job – as a 'half-timer'.

In 1882 the job of half-timing in a factory was common among boys in their early teens in Scotland. It meant that you went to school one day, and worked in the mill on the next. The chores in the mill involved a dozen hours of work a day. Mondays, Wednesdays and Fridays were spent collecting the tow in the flax mill, and Tuesdays, Thursdays and Saturdays sitting in the classroom of schoolmaster 'Stumpie' Bell in the academy, which was run by the owners of the mill.

Mr Bell was a strict schoolmaster. He had one leg shorter than the other, hence his nickname of 'Stumpie', for he literally stumped about as he moved across the classroom. He had a very nasty temper when angry, but he was always fair and just, much respected by the young Scots laddies. Some days the schoolboys would make fun of him. Harry never forgot the occasion he gave the rest of the class an impression of their master. 'Stumpie' came into the room and caught him at it. The punishment wasn't light!

Harry Lauder was one of about fifty 'half-timers' in that nineteenth-century flax-mill in the Scottish fishing town. In later life, when he was earning thousands, he often thought back to the pay he got in the mill. It was exactly two shillings and one penny a week, hardly enough to buy two or three newspapers by today's standards. Yet it could be spun out so much further in Lauder's boyhood.

Harry used to rise at five in the morning on Saturdays, and go the rounds as a delivery boy, handing about one hundred and fifty copies of the local newspaper, the *Arbroath Guide*, into various households. The ninepence a week he got for this additional task proved a useful bonus to the family budget.

Somehow, the Lauders survived this critical period in their lives. Harry's brother Matthew was growing up, and could take on an additional chore or two. Mrs Lauder went out to work at whatever jobs were offered her, just as so many hard-working thrifty Scottish mothers have done over the generations. Sometimes she would go out as a charwoman, washing and cleaning the homes of the richer citizens of Arbroath. On other occasions she would do a spot of 'baby-sitting', or go out to bake scones and bread for one of the wealthy mill-owners' wives.

A single penny earned was a penny gained, and very often saved, in those faraway times. The desires of the young were modest, totally removed in style from those of present over-coddled generations. At the end of the week a boy in nineteenth-century Scotland was given his 'Saturday penny'. It was a custom that survived well into the twentieth century. By today's standards a weekly pocket-money item of five shillings, or even ten, over a hundred times that amount, is quite normal.

Harry spent his Saturday penny on, of all things, tobacco. It was no sin for teenage laddies to smoke thick tobacco in the Scotland of the 1880s. They caught the habit from the hardy men they worked beside in the factories and at the docks. Lauder, a smoker all his life (how he loved the pipe in his days of retirement!), admitted that he was a very early slave to the smoking cult.

One day a travelling circus arrived in the little town of Arbroath, and cast a spell of magic over the poor laddies who worked so hard as 'half-timers' in the flax-mill and so diligently over their English grammar and arithmetic in the classroom. That circus, known as Ord's Circus, played a bigger part in influencing the Harry Lauder future than it has ever been given credit for. The lad didn't know it, but this was a turning-point in his life.

Harry was one of an unofficial committee elected by the schoolboys to seek a day off from the classroom so that they could enjoy a visit to the circus. But something went wrong; at the last minute the boys hesitated to make the request. Schoolmaster 'Stumpie' Bell, they felt, would never give his permission.

Nevertheless, visit the circus they did. A dozen of the lads, Harry included, played truant after lunchtime and went to the circus in the local park. They were in their seventh heaven, completely entranced by the colourful artistes and the animals. At night they watched the performance, thrilled and excited. This was another and wider world for the impressionable Harry Lauder. What a marvellous life these circus performers had! Imagine travelling the length and breadth of the land to create fun and gaiety – and getting paid for it, too! As he joined his chums to cheer the circus when it moved out from Arbroath at the weekend, Harry knew, deep down, that this could well be the life any boy would love to follow. Maybe even for himself? Or was it all too much to hope for?

The wrath of schoolmaster 'Stumpie' Bell was, of course, immense. Harry and his truant friends were given due physical punishment, and took it as bravely as they could. A regular 'stramash' ensued in the classroom, and someone – Lauder later recalled that it was probably himself – threw a school slate at the master, just missing his head by inches.

The Arbroath chapter in Lauder's life was, I am certain, his hardest and toughest. The work of teasing old ropes and ship's rigging into 'tow' and yarn to be mixed with flax often caused his fingers to bleed. And his mother's as well. The task was long and monotonous, and the sheer boredom of it all was killing. As Harry said in later life, many was the time that he cried with the sheer pain of it all. But his mother's happy, uncomplaining nature was a great encouragement to them both, and always, when the night's quota of work was tackled – sometimes very late into the night when the ropes and hawsers had been more difficult to tease than usual – they would kiss each other and cuddle up out of sheer thankfulness.

The Arbroath era in the Lauder saga is especially interesting because it served to introduce singing into his young life. As he sang so often on the stage in later years, *Singing Is The Thing That Mak's You Cheery*, and Harry certainly needed something to give him some cheer at this stage in his youth. He discovered that he was the owner of a quite melodious voice, and he started to learn a song or two. One in particular he liked, a rather sad song with the title *I'm A Gentleman Still*.

About this time, on his mother's instigation, Harry joined up in the Band of Hope. This was an organisation, very strong in Scotland, which campaigned for abstinence from the drinking of alcohol. Those who joined the Band became members of the proud Blue Ribbon Army, wore blue ribbons on their lapels, and held meetings where everybody sang hymns and encouraging and inspiring songs.

Youngsters were regarded as important recruits to the Band of Hope. They were regularly encouraged to stand up and sing a song, or give a recitation. The wholesome concert atmosphere prevailed; it was a most pleasant and innocuous evening.

One night, at such a meeting in Arbroath, Harry Lauder was persuaded to go on and 'sing something simple'. As he walked up, somewhat nervously, to the tiny platform, nobody in that gathering could have realised that this earnest Scottish schoolboy would one day become the greatest international entertainer in the world, with a magic drawing-power over audiences second to none.

All he could think of was *Bonnie Annie Laurie* and *I'm A Gentleman Still*. Suddenly there he was, aloft on the platform, and giving out with theses lines in his halting schoolboy voice:

> Though poverty daily looks in at my door,
> Though I'm hungry and footsore and ill,
> Thank God I can look the whole world in the face
> And say, I'm a Gentleman still!

Applause was music to young Lauder's ears, even so early. His fellow-members, schoolmates all, cheered and hand-clapped. He was the proudest wee laddie in the whole of Arbroath.

Fired with enthusiasm for the performing art, Harry started to become really interested in live concert-hall entertainment. A travelling party came to town in the following month, and advertised a 'grand amateur competition for ladies and gentlemen'. The top prizes were – real Abyssinian gold watches.

'Och, Harry, why don't you have a wee go?' urged his chums. 'You've as good as won it a'ready. Besides, you badly need a watch to mak' you keep good time at the mill!'

There were over a dozen rivals to Lauder in that contest, but he won the day and carried off a gold watch for his prize. Once again he featured the same song, *I'm A Gentleman Still*. It was proving his lucky song, as dozens of other songs were to prove his lucky ones in later life. That gold watch was a keepsake of Lauder's all his life.

In the audience that evening at the concert in Arbroath was the manager of the flax-mill where young Lauder worked. He was so glad to see one of his own 'half-timers' win that he sent round a shilling backstage and added his compliments.

'Aye, Harry lad, you'll be gettin' five pounds a week afore you dee if you gang on at this rate!' They were to be prophetic words.

His boyhood chums congratulated him. He kept up the good work, and within another six weeks had taken part in a similar competition and, once more, carried off the top prize, this time a six-bladed knife. He later sold it to a man in his mill for elevenpence, being already the proud owner of a knife which he had saved up to buy. Thus early did he show his Scottish business acumen.

At the ripe young age of thirteen little Harry Lauder from the wee town of Arbroath was already shaping right brawly as an entertainer. And making money as one, too!

Harry was only fourteen when his family moved from the east coast of Scotland into the 'Black Country' of Lanarkshire and the coal mines around Hamilton. It was a busy wee Scots town, with a population of about forty thousand in those days, and with work in the coal mines the main industry. A lad like 'Wee Harry', as he was known, could earn all of fifteen shillings a week for being a trapper. This meant that he had to open and close the wooden gates controlling the air currents to the mines. It wasn't long before he graduated to be a pony driver, and was earning a pound a week.

It was hard work for the lad, but he had to look after his widowed mother and the rest of the family in the years before his own marriage. He worked long hours and hard, and the money, though small, was always needed at the end of each week.

In surroundings like these – bleak, dull and quite unglamorous – a man has to joke and see the lighter side if he wants to get through the week without going under. In every country people brought up in poor circumstances usually see more fun in the world than those with an easier life. They crack gags and jokes, and laugh at the little things. Doubtless this is why most of the comedians in the world have come from poor backgrounds. So it was natural that young Lauder, as he slogged away in the pits of Lanarkshire, in central Scotland, should joke and laugh and sing. These soggy pits were drab and often dismal places.

'Let's hae a wee sang, Harry ma lad!' his fellow-miners encouraged him. Two of them in particular, Jimmy McCulloch and Rab MacBeth, kept asking him to sing up; he had the kind of voice that made them cheery at work.

This is exactly how Harry Lauder was launched into becoming an entertainer. He sang down the mine, and gained a fair reputation. His first public appearance in the Hamilton district came in yet another Band of Hope concert, and once again, just as he had done at Arbroath, he sang the song *I'm A Gentleman Still*.

As he progressed through life, Lauder was to remember clearly these hard, tough, back-breaking days in the coal mines of Scotland. The memory of them would flash back as he went out before sophisticated audiences, from New York to London, and told them what a fine thing it was to sing, how it brightened everything when life seemed dark and dreary, and how singing was the ideal thing to make a man feel cheery.

This was exactly the philosophy he had adopted – but of necessity – in the coal mines and, as the weeks passed, Harry Lauder became famed locally around Hamilton as a comic singer. One night Rab MacBeth, from the mine, ran a 'Grand Competition Concert', and Harry was easily persuaded to take part. He was rather enjoying the sense of competition by now. It was a boisterous audience, with some of the rougher and wilder lads in the town in to see what they could make of it. Several of the acts that went on before Lauder didn't quite make it with this element, and were booed off the stage. Harry's nervousness increased.

The situation grew quite dangerous a few minutes before Harry was due on. There were many cat-calls from the audience, and a handful had to be shown to the door. In fact, big Rab MacBeth had to go on to the stage and offer to fight any man in the hall if the outcry continued.

Then the Lauder act was announced. Harry strode on, gallant as ever, and went right into his routine of patter and song. There was a hush, the tough boys listened, and then . . . applause, applause. He had won through to make a decided impression with his cheery songs and humour. And the entire audience liked what he did.

Well, that night, I believe, really decided it. Lauder made up his mind that he would give up his work in the pits, and turn professional as a singer-comedian. He felt that this was really the life he should lead. Besides, there was more money in it if you succeeded!

His professional début was in the village of Larkhall, in Lanarkshire. The fee he received was the handsome one of five shillings. How he treasured that first bit of professional earning! He was to go out on to worldwide stages and earn thousands of pounds and dollars in future years, but that well-earned five shillings was the fee he appreciated most.

'Aye, there's something in this game,' he told himself. 'Here they are, ready and willing tae pay me for singing for them. I can do this all over Scotland. I'll sing my heart out for this. No, no . . . no more giving my performances free. If anybody asks me to do a turn, it's five shillings or nothing at all.'

One Saturday evening he did his song-and-comedy act in the Lanarkshire town of Motherwell. It went over well. So well, in fact, that he decided that he would enter the following week for a comedy-singing contest under the auspices of the Glasgow Harmonic Society. This was progress. It marked his first appearance in the big city of Glasgow and, it proved successful, too. Harry walked home with the second prize of the night, and an engagement in three variety halls as well. A single pound was thrown in as a bonus.

It was the proudest moment and conquest of his career so far. Harry took the money and went out and bought himself an astrakhan collar for his coat. This astrakhan collar, he felt, was the ultimate sign of the real and genuine actor. It was the badge of profession for the true and dedicated actor and performer. But Harry, the ex-pitboy from Hamilton, was as entitled to it as anyone, he kept telling himself. Now he was 'one of yon actor chappies'.

Becoming a professional – as he was from the year 1894 – paid off. Glasgow dates were offered to him. He was booked for the Scotia Music-hall, a small variety theatre where the reputations of many performers had been made. It was an event in any young artiste's career to be seen at the Scotia. If the audience reacted favourably, you got a full week's engagement. If they didn't, you were tossed out on your ear, astrakhan collar and all! But, either way, and if nobody else wanted to know you, there was really nothing to lose.

Harry Lauder played this date, and was asked to accept a full week's work. As long as he lived he never forgot this very first public appearance at the old Scotia. He had just gone on and was doing his well-known 'walk-round' when a man in the gallery shouted: 'Ach, awa' back tae the pit, Harry, man!' Luckily, Lauder never took that customer's advice, although it did disconcert him somewhat. But he stuck to the showbusiness game, and found it sticking, in turn, to him.

Next, he appeared at shows sponsored by the Glasgow Harmonic Society, where he had already won a competition. This was a temperance organisation which offered tea and a Scotch cookie on Saturday nights, along with live entertainment. It was free-and-easy entertainment, not unlike that which is now being offered in the pubs and working-men's clubs of Britain.

Touring days came after this. Harry signed to go out in a company along with the famous Scottish violinist Mackenzie Murdoch and, in 1896, at the age of twenty-five, he left home on a tour of Scotland. This came to be known as the Harry Lauder-Mackenzie Murdoch tour. and on their first trip around they lost over a hundred and fifty pounds. But that story can wait till the next chapter.

Lauder was now earning thirty-five shillings a week for his act on tour. He did only three songs a night, and didn't consider himself poorly paid. Once, doing a comic act in Glasgow, and facing ominous silence from the audience, he was wondering where on earth he could escape to when his false moustache began to droop and slide down. As it finally came off, there was a loud laugh from the audience.

Deciding it was the only thing he could do, Harry Lauder played up to that laughter response. It brought the audience into a mood of great geniality and friendliness.

The proprietress, Mrs Bayliss, came round and said: 'Do that every night, Harry, please. It's a hit; they love it.'

That incident with the moustache made Harry, in later years, buy himself what he called a 'movable moustache'. It proved a far better sticker, even though it hurt his face like nothing on earth.

Reading the Glasgow *Evening Citizen* one night, after a show in the city, he chanced on an advertisement asking for a comedian. It offered a six-weeks' season with a concert party. It was a job that called for someone of many parts and talents. The man who filled the post would have to be baggage-man, billposter, stage carpenter and much more, all for thirty-five shillings a week.

Harry applied for the job and got it. He toured for six busy weeks, opening at Beith, in Ayrshire. Then came his first engagement in English variety. He signed a contract to tour the Moss and Thornton halls in the north of England, ending up with a fortnight back in Glasgow at the Scotia and the Gaiety theatres. During this period he made his first appearance in the city of Carlisle, several miles over the Scottish border from Gretna playing in a variety show at the old Public Hall.

The ex-miner lad with the impressive astrakhan collar was now firmly committed to the glamorous, exciting and wonderful world of showbusiness. He was anxious, insecure – but full of enthusiasm. There could be no turning back now. It was win or lose, and the big wide world awaited him. The sky was the limit for a chap with both guts and talent.

Harry knew he simply had to succeed. Besides, he was now married to the nicest Scots lass in the world. . . .

The Lass he Loved

EVERY LADDIE LOVES a lassie! This was the ever-present and recurring theme in the songs that Harry Lauder wrote and sang and made famous. A list of his love songs surpasses in quantity any similar listing in modern-day hit parades.

There is, of course, his very own Top of the Tartan pops – *I Love A Lassie*, first sung in a pantomime at the old Theatre Royal in Glasgow, and written by Harry himself in collaboration with his friend Gerald Grafton. There is also *She Is My Rosie*, and *Queen Amang The Heather*, and *She's The Lass For Me*, and *Bonnie Wee Annie*. They all had a grand lilt in them.

Harry also sang, often, that *It's Nice When You Love A Wee Lassie*. Not far behind in popularity came *I Wish I Had Someone To Love Me!* Love, romance, bonnie lassies, and romantic walks over the heather and by the loch-side. These were the simple ingredients of many of his lyrics. Love, he used to sing, 'is the sunshine o' a bonnie lass's smile'. Harry Lauder realised this full well himself, for he had personal experience of his own bonnie wee lass.

Her name was Annie Vallance, but her friends knew her as Nancy. She lived in Hamilton, the mining centre to which Harry and his family moved after their Arbroath days, and she was a singing member of the Salvation Army in the town. Talk about modern teenage romances! Nancy was only fourteen – a bonnie and mature fourteen, to be sure – when she knocked young Lauder completely 'tapsalteerie', as he put it afterwards. This is a

...rd which can be translated as 'putting you into

...oung love at a Salvation Army meeting in the
...unday afternoon. The introduction was effected
... younger brothers, Tom Vallance. Like Harry,
...nines. The Lauder lad really fell for the girl. He
...p nor eat for thinking of her.

...Lauder matured quickly in the 1880s. Life was
...They became men at fifteen or sixteen, and
...rs down the coal mines.

...e was the eldest of her family. Her father was
...and he happened to be the underground man-
...even Pit, in the Quarter, a village near Hamilton.
...ally the boss's daughter. Young Lauder decided
...er first. He caught him in a leisure moment and
told him. 'Master Vallance, I'm verra much in love wi' your
Nance. In fact, I'm tellin' you, I'd verra much like to marry her.'
The pair of them – pit manager and employee – adjourned to a
nearby hostelry, and Vallance gave his consent.

'But mind, you'll hae tae ask Nance's mother first,' he advised
the young man.

Harry went next day to call on Mrs Vallance, and found that
his supposedly secret ambition was no secret with her. With true
feminine instinct, she had guessed many weeks before that the
Lauder lad was in love with her daughter. Lauder, ever the gallant,
said his ambition was to make Nancy into a great lady, with the
best clothes and a carriage and a big house. Again, prophetic
words.

Their courtship was a brief one, and with the wedding day set
they started looking for a house, and one suddenly became vacant
in a miners' row of houses controlled by the owners of the colliery.
So Harry Lauder was given a house at the comfortable rent of

three shillings and sixpence a week. The money was kept off his weekly pay; he was now earning about three pounds a week, and had over twenty pounds in the bank. He wasn't doing too badly, compared with his earlier days in the flax-mill.

Nance and Harry had their little home re-painted and papered. It was their first home together, and it was a palace to them both. They were married in midsummer, on the 18th June 1890. Harry was nineteen years old now. The wedding took place in the home of the Vallance family in The Bent, in Hamilton, and the parlour table served as the altar.

Their wedding was what they called in the Scotland of last century a 'pay-wedding'. That's to say, all the outside guests paid for their tickets. A double ticket cost eight shillings and sixpence. This meant that they could really 'go to town' with the festivities at the wedding reception in the Lesser Victoria Hall.

The food was out of this world for a humble mining family. The two families had thought of everything. There was steak pie, potatoes, rice pudding, tea, pastry-cakes, and lots of beer. Oh, and there was Scotch whisky for the top table. The Best Man was Harry's brother Matthew, and the Best Maid was Nance's sister Kate. There were speeches and toasts, and the chairman sang an Irish song, *Norah, The Pride o' Kildare*.

Naturally, they called on the bridegroom. Harry, fond of singing, stood up with a great big smile and treated the guests to his versions of *Bonnie Annie Laurie* and *Scotland Yet*, a redoubtable combination. Others sang more songs, both Scottish and Irish, and some gave recitations. Everybody danced and sang into the wee sma' hours – until it was 4 am and the dawn.

Other folk might hold grander weddings, and in more stately surroundings, but to the Lauders and the Vallances the union of Harry and Nancy was the happiest wedding for a generation, and one they would remember all their lives.

34

Long honeymoons were not in fashion in Harry and Nancy Lauder's time. There was work to do, and newly-married men got little time for holidays, so Harry and his bride took a one-day honeymoon, and they spent it in dear old Glasgow town, the big city on the doorstep of Hamilton. They wandered past the big shops, hand in hand, and then went off on a visit to McLeod's Wax Works in the Trongate, where they saw the effigies of the notorious body-snatchers, Burke and Hare, and of various robbers and murderers. It was the 'done thing' to pay such a visit to the wax works, even on a honeymoon. Then the newly-weds set off for a ride on the top-deck of a Glasgow tramcar, and journeyed as far as the gates of Barlinnie Prison. They ended the day with a stroll along the Broomielaw, by the banks of the River Clyde.

By the Monday Harry Lauder had discarded his wedding-day togs, and was back in miner's clothes, digging for coal in Allantown Colliery.

Harry and Nancy were, of course, very much in love, and he never regretted his choice. He often said it was a true case of love at first sight, and repeatedly told how he fell head-over-heels in love with this blue-eyed lassie from Lanarkshire. He knew it was a case of rushing into marriage, but he had the secure feeling that this was 'for keeps', as indeed it proved. In Nancy Vallance, he said in later life, he gained the truest friend of a whole lifetime, and an inspiration for his work.

On his various tours of America, Harry often talked to audiences about his Nance, and she did, in fact, accompany him on many of the tours. The American people liked to hear the Scot tell their true love-story. He used to joke from the stage of the biggest theatres in America that he had been coming there for twenty years and – 'Here, I'm tellin' you somethin', it's juist a wee secret between you an' me, remember-r-r . . . but . . . I've always brought the same wee wifie wi' me!'

Harry knew that all the world loved a lover, and that songs about love awoke a chord in every person's heart.

He used to give, freely, this advice to young men in love like himself: 'Dinna ca' canny, laddie. Love can be the greatest thing in any man's life, and it's well worth the effort to get your share o' it.

'Once you know your mind, laddie, dinna hesitate one meenit . . . !'

The thriving wee towns of Scotland have never boasted of bright lights, glittering theatre canopies, night-clubs or lavish stage spectaculars. Not for them the super-duper style of entertainment, à la Broadway or West End! Small cinemas (many now, alas, disappearing or gone for good) and the local hall have been more typical of showbusiness in this rural belt.

But the local town-hall concert has always had one great virtue. Many of the artistes who eventually go on to make a national name – in theatre, cinema or on television – often get their early start in these small-town concerts. They are fine try-out ground for artistes making their way in the business.

Many of these concerts are still staged today, even in an age that is crazy over television. In fact, I often feel it is a pity that radio and television producers, and other talent scouts, don't have sufficient time to take a look at some of them, and discover a sprinkling of worthwhile talent for the future. These concerts, and the cabaret shows staged in hundreds of clubs up and down Britain, are the only 'nursery' left for the all-consuming market of entertainment.

Towards the end of last century Harry Lauder was active at these concerts in the towns of Scotland. His fee was five shillings a night, and sometimes ten shillings. And he proved well worth the money, for most of the people in these small-town audiences liked the type of songs and comedy he provided.

Around the mid-1890s – in the autumn of 1896, to be precise – Harry was asked to join Mr Donald Munro's North Concert Party and to tour with it through the north and central areas of Scotland.

'I'll pay you six pounds a week, lad,' said Donald, and it was a deal. The show played to well-filled halls up and down the Highlands, and the profits were obviously considerable.

On the same bill was Mackenzie Murdoch, easily the most skilled violinist in Scotland at that time.

One night he approached young Lauder, and suggested that they might go out on their own during the next summer season, and see if they couldn't 'make a bob or two'. They would, in other words, become their own promoters, and reap the benefit of the profits, average or high.

'Aye, a grand idea!' said Harry. 'Let's try it, Mac.' And both of them shook hands on it and said their farewells, with great goodwill, to their old employer, Donald Munro, from Aberdeenshire.

Out on their own the following summer, Lauder and Murdoch began to see exactly how much risk there was in this business of promoting their own stage tours. But not until after they had, too optimistically, visualised huge profits, working on the rash assumption that every hall would be packed to capacity.

Ah, the perils and dangers of being an impresario! Even on this small scale they could be considerable.

The two artistes had special posters printed, with the bold heading LAUDER-MURDOCH CONCERT PARTY. Then, with high hope in their hearts, but pockets scarce of silver, they set out to distribute them round the towns on their tour's itinerary.

It was the August of 1897. And what better day to open the tour than the August Bank Holiday, with every member of the population wondering how he or she could spend the evening!

The artistes knew no modesty in their billings. Harry himself had been so enamoured of how a local newspaper writer had described him some weeks previously that he used his flowery description and billed himself as – HARRY LAUDER, 'Scotland's Pride'. Mackenzie Murdoch was proclaimed as THE WORLD'S GREATEST FIDDLER.

The singer was a tenor named Scott Rae, the girl vocalist a soprano with the good Scottish name of Flora Donaldson, and the unit was completed by a ventriloquist named Howard, who had the temerity – though so far away from base – to describe himself as 'London's Star Ventriloquist'.

Lauder and Murdoch made a bargain to take five pounds weekly each out of the box-office takings. Another eight pounds was to pay for the wages of the other three artistes in the company. The rest – well, it was to be the profit.

Alas, the customers didn't come in as they had anticipated. The people of Kilmarnock, in Ayrshire, couldn't have cared less. Neither could the good folk of Irvine, Kilwinning, Saltcoats, Troon and Ayr, entertainment hungry though they might be.

The only profit came in the fourth week of the tour, and a slump set in for the final two. One night business was so bad there were hardly twenty-five people in the hall. The following evening only eleven turned up, and so many of these had complimentary tickets that the box-office notched up only one shilling and nine-pence.

Poor Harry Lauder was in a sizzling temper, which wasn't part of his nature. He even did something that he would never have done in more experienced days; he went on-stage in one central Scottish town and reprimanded the inhabitants for not flocking in by the hundred to enjoy so fine and star-studded a concert party.

Between them, Lauder and Murdoch, comedian and violinist,

lost what was 'a packet' for those days through their concert-promoting venture. They returned to base in Glasgow two hundred pounds the poorer. By the following summer, when they tried again, the two artistes had learned the value of that old adage 'It Pays to Advertise'. They trebled their budget on bill-posting and publicity, and began to pull in many more customers, sometimes even capacity houses. The profits for this tour amounted to over two hundred pounds, so Lauder and Murdoch really came out even after two years.

Now the people in the smaller Scottish towns and villages, and even in the cities, were beginning to get to know the two showmen who were so determined to thrust their talent upon them. Summertime tours over two years earned Lauder and Murdoch some six hundred pounds, and profits were high in cities like Edinburgh and Dundee. Life was smiling for them both again.

Harry Lauder's brother-in-law, Tom Vallance, was called in about this time to join the tour as manager and general cashier. He was given the task of looking after the money and counting the total profits – or losses – each night. It was to be his first task in management, and something he was going to sample to a much greater degree in the years ahead in the great big outside world of international showbusiness.

There was hardly a town in Scotland that didn't have the honour of a visit at this time from the Lauder-Murdoch Concert Party. Harry and his good friend Mac had many adventures 'on the road', just as artistes have, even today, when they venture on tour through the Highlands and islands of Scotland.

Many amusing incidents occurred in connection with lodgings in tiny rooms, or where elderly Scots landladies feared the arrival of ghosts and spirits. Theatrical boarders were always slightly madcap, at least in the eyes of douce citizens in the smaller towns.

When their tour touched the extreme south of Scotland, Lauder

39

and his partner ventured over the border into England, playing in the small towns in Cumberland and Northumberland, and in the city of Carlisle. This was a new experience for them, and Lauder began to notice that audiences, even those over the Scotland-England border, were really the same wherever you went. These Sassenachs were not so much different in taste and outlook from the slightly sterner Scotsman up north.

It made Harry ponder . . . and a bright new plan came into his inventive mind.

To London – in Yellow Spats and Astrakhan

CONTRACTS ARE A necessity in the world of showbusiness. It can so often become a cut-throat game, with impresarios and theatre owners taking such chances on the popularity of a production that they can win or lose quite considerable sums of money. So it pays every performer to have his or her terms and conditions of work put on a strictly legal basis.

Occasionally, but very occasionally, instances occur in theatre where nobody signs a contract. The artiste trusts the producer of the show, and the producer trusts the artiste. They can be such good friends of long standing that they dismiss entirely the idea of a legal contract.

The story of Harry Lauder's friendship with an English theatre-owner, Denis Clarke, of the Argyle Theatre in Birkenhead, on Merseyside, is an almost classic instance of how theatre manager and artiste respected each other implicitly, with Clarke forgetting the original terms of the contract and deciding to pay Harry Lauder what he felt he was worth.

The Argyle Theatre in Birkenhead was a real turning-point in Lauder's early career. It was a true music-hall of Victorian England, and flourished for seventy-two years as a popular hall of variety performers. Originally, it had been a sort of public house-hostelry, with entertainers doing their act in a hall connected to the drinking lounge. The customers sat round at tables, and ate and drank and were merry. Artistes liked the carefree, impromptu style of the place, not unlike many English music-halls of the period. What's more, the patrons were usually in a most receptive mood and knew how to enjoy themselves.

The Argyle first started two years before Harry Lauder was born in 1870, and had featured a small boy named Dan Leno in its first Christmas pantomime; he was the same Dan Leno who was to grow up to become one of England's greatest music-hall stars.

Denis J Clarke took over the running of the Birkenhead music-hall from his uncle, Denis Grannell, gave it the name of the Argyle, and nursed it into a great and popular theatre, with a real auditorium and seating. He also had a knack of spotting future 'greats' among unknown performers playing his hall.

Like all showbusiness, the Argyle had its ups and downs, and Denis Clarke had to be alive to every situation, especially when rival shows such as a travelling circus came to town in the December of 1896. He kept reaching for new ideas in showmanship, and was one of the first English showmen, in fact, to present a primitive style of motion picture on a screen which hung halfway down the auditorium.

One day Denis Clarke heard of a young man from Scotland who was said to be very good as an Irish comedian. Apparently he sang songs with a genuine Irish flavour and could alter his own Scottish dialect and accent to talk in the attractive brogue of the Emerald Isle.

'The name is Lauder . . . Harry Lauder,' a friend in the business whispered to him. 'He's quite a novelty. You should have a look at him, Denis.'

Being a showman with a liking for novelties, Denis went north to see the performer, and booked him. So, in the week of the 13th June 1898 – he was twenty-seven at the time – Harry Lauder arrived at Birkenhead, nearly half-a-century before any of the Beatles were born in this, their home neighbourhood, and proceeded to offer the customers at the Argyle a music-hall act composed entirely of Irish songs.

The region around the Mersey has always been one in sympathy with Ireland, doubtless because of its sea links with Dublin and Belfast, and many in the audience that night had Irish associations. Irish songs and comedy were a sure-fire item for applause at the Argyle. Harry Lauder, an unknown, went on stage and started his act. He gave the audience one Irish song after another, and proved a tremendous hit. The customers liked him so much they kept calling 'Encore', and refused to let him go.

Denis Clarke, realising he had a hit on his hands, rushed backstage and asked the little Scotsman to go on and make a second appearance. Lauder looked taken aback and somewhat surprised. He frowned.

'I'm sorry, Maister Clarke, but I juist canna do it. You see . . .' he paused dramatically – 'the truth is, I've nae mair Irish songs.'

Clarke was worried. 'But surely, Mr Lauder, you make more than one appearance up in Scotland and its music-halls?'

'Aye, but that's different,' replied Harry. 'In Scotland, you see, I'm a Scotch comedian. But doon here . . . weel, it's different. You see, my songs are too broad for them. They widna' understand me.'

Alert to every situation, Denis Clarke turned on the wee Scot and cried: 'Never mind. Tonight, Lauder, try them . . . try your Scotch songs, for goodness sake, and see what happens.'

He was adamant that Lauder must go on for a second appearance that night. In fact, the audience could be clearly heard by the artistes backstage. They kept calling and shouting for another turn by the 'young Irishman'. Little did Harry Lauder know, as he hesitated in the wings, that it was to prove a vital night in his life and career.

He went on for a second appearance, swung into a simple

43

Scottish melody, followed with another – and was a sensation. The audience of happy Merseysiders rose to these refreshing songs about the land to the north of England. They couldn't get enough of this unknown laddie.

It was theatre history in the making. The box-office was jammed by the demand for seats.

Denis Clarke paid Harry Lauder four pounds for that week, and booked him for a quick return after his next (and already contracted) Scottish tour. Then he persuaded him to sign a contract guaranteeing a booking every six months over a lengthy period. Lauder's salary was to start at eight pounds a week and rise to fifteen.

The significant thing about that midsummer week's music-hall in one of England's most famous theatres in 1898 was that it gave young Lauder a new confidence in his act of portraying a Scotsman. He realised its potential from that night on. Until that evening he had been confining himself to Scotland and the extreme north of England, touring with concert parties. Now he made a key decision. From that moment on he would stop being an Irishman on the stage, and would become a Scotch-style comedian.

It was, when you consider it, a quite momentous decision. The mere chance by which it happened proves that luck and the turn of events often play a larger part in all our lives than most of us realise.

That memorable night at the Birkenhead theatre started a lifelong friendship between the Clarke family of the Argyle and Harry Lauder and his family. For the next forty years Harry Lauder went back, time and again, to the little Argyle Theatre, and Denis Clarke, forgetting the terms of their original contract, generously paid the Scot more and more each time, knowing his real worth and drawing power. The Clarkes were generous and honest men.

Harry Lauder, in his turn, reciprocated. Once, even when there was no clause in his contract stipulating it, he travelled all the way from America merely to play a date at the Argyle. His previous contract had expired, but he trusted the Clarkes.

'I'll never forget the wee Argyle Theatre or my friends, the Clarkes,' he used to say. 'They turned me from bein' an Irishman into a Scotsman, somethin' I was all the time. And they gave me confidence to go further south to London.'

All the famous ones of the English music-hall, from Marie Lloyd to Vesta Tilley, appeared at the Birkenhead Argyle, and two years after Harry Lauder came a dancing troupe known as 'The Eight Lancashire Lads'. One of its members was a young lad later to achieve world renown as Charlie Chaplin. He was later to become a close personal friend of Harry Lauder, welcoming him on several occasions to the film studios in Hollywood.

The great Billie Burke, famed on American stage and screen, also adorned that early English music-hall stage. She visited Birkenhead as one third of an act billed as Burke, Andrus and Frisco. Frisco was a performing mule, and Adru Andrus was Billie's father. Billie often talked of how she recited Rudyard Kipling's *The Absent-Minded Beggar* that week at the Argyle, and was paid the handsome (for those days) salary of a guinea for doing so.

News that saddened Harry Lauder's heart in later life, when he was retired and living quietly in Scotland as Sir Harry, came in the autumn of 1940. A letter from Birkenhead told him that German bombers, in a raid over the Mersey, had dropped their weapons on Merseyside and had directly hit the gallant little music-hall, sending it up in flames.

His thoughts went back forty-two years to that June evening of 1898 when he had realised for the first time the attraction of Scottish songs with audiences who lived far from the Highland hills and lochs. He recalled the excitement of that evening. It had been one of the turning points of his showbusiness career.

Success with songs and comedy about the Highlands, the kind of success he had just met with on Merseyside, set Harry thinking hard about his next move.

The Scot has often made his mark in business, both in London and in countries overseas. But the Scottish music-hall comedian, unfortunately, has never been so successful. Somehow, not many have tackled the southward road from Glasgow to the West End, even in modern times.

The failure of a few has, no doubt, had much to do with this omission. 'Why try when others have failed?' say comedians who stay at home. In fact, singers from Scotland have proved notably more successful than their funnymen colleagues from the land of Auld Lang Syne.

Another reason, of course, is that theatre work in Scotland has been able to absorb the efforts of the country's native comedians for the greater part of each year. Pantomime seasons start early at Christmastime and sometimes don't finish until the end of March. Short revue seasons fill in the interval. Then it's time to launch into the summer seasons, which often continue right through to October. By the time a Scots comedian has sought some rest and sunshine, usually on the Spanish island of Majorca, it is his cue for winter revue or pantomime again.

Many people outside Scotland blame the Scottish dialect for the fact that so few of their laughter-rousing countrymen ever star in London. They maintain that it is difficult for southerners to understand fully what the kilted comedian is talking about. Harry Lauder, after successes in his own country, faced the same philosophy. He knew personally several comedians of his own race who had gone to London and failed to register. They had come home with their ego and enthusiasm very much deflated.

He was doing very nicely, thank you, in his own land and with audiences who knew what he was talking and singing about. But he was soon to be jolted out of his complacency and content. In fact, his experience at the Argyle in Birkenhead had already done this in part.

A visit to the old Empire Theatre in Glasgow suddenly changed his way of thinking – almost overnight. He went as a member of the audience. The famous Dan Leno, one of the kings of the English music-hall, was starring. This visit by Lauder proved true inspiration. He watched closely, marvelled – and thought hard. Now, if this chap Dan Leno could get a hundred pounds a week for singing London-style songs up here in Scotland, then surely a fellow named Harry Lauder could get the same for singing Scottish songs in London. It was a point worth thinking about.

On to that Glasgow stage, with a tough and laugh-hungry audience waiting, came Dan Leno, and gave them his famous *Shopwalker* song. Harry enjoyed his Cockney patter; what's more, he understood it. So did most of the audience around him.

Lauder kept his thoughts to himself, but, inwardly, he was highly excited. Why, he kept saying, couldn't equally amusing comedy songs by a Scotsman, and about Scotsmen in general, click in the theatres in London? He rushed home and told Nance of his idea. He shared all his ideas with her. Briefly, his plan was to keep himself clear of a fortnight's engagements in Scotland and try himself out in the London music-halls. He was sure he could win success.

So confident was Lauder, in fact, that, when he got to the Central Station in Glasgow, he asked for a single ticket only – third-class, of course! If he made the grade, as he hoped, there would be no immediate need for a return ticket.

The date was the 19th March, the year 1900. Harry was twenty-nine, and full of hope and ideas. He and Nance kept their savings in a stocking in a secret spot beneath the bed in the kitchen. Harry went to this and took out twenty pounds in golden sovereigns. Then he said goodbye to Nance. He wanted little talk of his 'invasion' of London, and he wanted nobody to see him off at the station. There must be absolutely no fuss.

What a character! What a sight he must have been! He was dressed in a pair of tartan trousers, with yellow spats, and brown boots, and he wore a coloured waistcoat and a black frock-coat. His collar stood up with large square peaks. His tie was a loud pattern of black-and-green. To cap it all, he sported a tile hat that was a very bad fit, and over his arm he carried his precious coat with the astrakhan collar, the one that so proudly marked him out as an 'actor laddie'.

There was no doubt about it. Harry Lauder, the ex-miner, was out to impress London, and maybe the world as well. Arriving at Euston Station, he got off the train and found little groups of Londoners stopping to stare at him. Well they might! He made a truly comical figure in that get-up.

Harry hadn't the nerve to try the more imposing-looking hotels. He booked in at a shabby-looking boarding-house in the Euston Road, and settled for a room that would give him bed-and-breakfast for three shillings and sixpence. He had to be thrifty and canny; London, by Scottish standards, was an awfully expensive place.

So he started the tiring round of variety agents' offices, an experience that so many performers all round the world know so well. He remembered the advice his closer friends back home had handed out to him. A few, only a few, were in on the secret of his trip south. 'Remember-r-r, Harry Lad,' they had told him. 'Spend as little time as possible in London. It's a hard city, and there's nae silver on the streets, like folk say. Get back over the Border as quickly as you can!'

Lauder, however, had guts, He had faced setbacks and disappointments from schooldays. Not one, not even a score of rebuffs in that first week, was going to set him back on the road to the north again.

In blasé mood, the hardened variety agents listened to his tale and to stories of his success in Scotland.

'But you're new, son,' they told him. 'You're a completely unknown quantity down here. How do we know you'll be worth taking a chance on?'

It was the age-old story, heard from Broadway to Leicester Square to Melbourne. Nobody wants to know a performer who is an 'unknown quantity'. Yet how can he prove himself unless the unexpected chance arrives?

Harry got chatting with a veteran variety agent, Walter Munroe. He at least listened and tried to help the Scot. The first of Harry's precious golden sovereigns came out, and he boldly bought Walter a drink in a nearby hostelry. Still nothing was forthcoming in the way of bookings. Two days later Lauder was walking along the Strand with Munroe when up came Tom Tinsley, a well-known theatreman, who managed Gatti's-in-the-Road, a little music-hall. They exchanged courtesies, and Harry was introduced.

The three men adjourned to a nearby saloon bar, and Tinsley and Munroe started the usual 'shop-talk'. Every now and then Lauder chipped in with an observation. Then he put his hand in his sporran and brought out the second of those golden sovereigns. After all, a man had to impress, even though he had no dates in his book. The gesture impressed Tinsley. Imagine a poor Scotsman being so rich! He must have a worthwhile act. The agent made a mental note of the name.

It went on like this for almost a week. A depressing, frustrating week. Harry now had cheap lodgings in the Lambeth Road area, a shabby, poorly-furnished room on the third floor. It was costing him fifteen shillings a week. A less determined type would have given up the ghost. There was every opportunity for Lauder to sit down, think too hard, and commiserate with himself over his lack of luck. But not our Harry. He had known too many set-backs, and he knew the right way was to go in there fighting, full of bounce and hope. He used to get up at six in the morning, eat a meagre breakfast, and walk into the heart of London. He was always in the variety agents' quarter bright and early, ready to plod round searching for work. In the evening he would walk home to the Lambeth Road, and anxiously ask the landlady for letters or messages. Invariably, there were none.

Days passed. Days of tedious waiting and near-despair. Then, suddenly, there was a spark of hope. Tired and weary after another day's plodding, Harry arrived back at his 'digs' in the evening and was told: 'There's a telegram in your room, Mr Lauder.'

A telegram! He could scarcely dare to hope. Harry Lauder climbed those stairs to the third floor, four at a time. He launched himself to his room. Yes, there it lay all right. 'Mr H Lauder', it said, on the envelope. His hand shook with excitement as he tore it open, and read:

ONE OF MY TURNS ILL STOP CAN YOU DEPUTISE AT TEN O'CLOCK TONIGHT? REPLY AT ONCE TINSLEY GATTI'S.

Could he deputise? Lauder couldn't wait to say 'I will'. He dashed down the stairs, rushed to a nearby shop telephone, and called up Tom Tinsley, telling him enthusiastically he would be happy to appear.

This was yet another magic moment in time for Harry. Here

he was, in London town, and the chance he had dreamed about awaited. He was so thrilled and excited he went into a grocer's shop, bought a fivepenny tin of salmon, and went home to his 'digs' and celebrated – with the salmon, some bread and butter, and a hot pot of tea. Not even the most expensive of dinners in later life could have tasted as good.

As he ate his bread and salmon, Lauder thought out his act. He decided he would do the song *Tobermory*. It had so much gusto and humour. Besides, he knew it best. He would follow with *The Lass O' Killiecrankie.* a rollicking and jolly number, and then he would swing into his Irish character number, *Calligan Call Again!*

Oh! the joy of anticipation. And the fear of it, too! Harry set out from his humble lodgings and got to the theatre nearly two hours before he was due on. His nerves were taut and near to breaking point. At one moment he thought he was going to faint. He thought of Nance up in Scotland, patiently waiting for news. He thought of his triumphs in Glasgow and district. He thought of Dan Leno and how he had daringly and so confidently tackled that audience at the Glasgow Empire.

Now he was on. It had seemed like a lifetime. The stage-hands, curious, stood and watched this odd-looking Scot. He could see the audience, not too large but interested. He could hear a few giggles. Then some laughs. Then – bless 'em – more laughs. The initial silence had been almost unbearable. But now they were thawing. He sang *Tobermory*, and finished it to warm applause. The stage-manager dropped the curtain, but the clapping continued. He could scarcely believe his good fortune. Those Londoners were actually asking for more.

Harry hirpled cheekily on-stage again. This time he gave them *The Lass O' Killiecrankie*, a number written and composed entirely by himself. It was all about his favourite Jane McPhail, 'as sweet as honey dew, the lass o' Killiecrankie'.

'Encore!' the audience at Gatti's shouted. 'Encore!' Harry was gathering confidence now, and he launched into his Irish character song *Calligan, Call Again!*, the number he had written with Herbert Rutter. It had the audience laughing heartily as he recounted his adventures in buying a pair of pants from a tailor named Calligan and having to take them off when he couldn't pay the bill.

Simple, almost naive stuff by today's comparison, and much of it not even good verse. But Harry could put such fun and pathos into it, and spice it all with that famous Lauder chuckle. He made the most of even poor material, surrounding it with his own personal magic.

The audience certainly loved him that night he deputised at Gatti's. So much so that he had to go on and make a little speech of thanks.

'Thank you, kind folks, thank you,' he said. 'I'm tellin' you, the name is Harry Lauder, an' I want you to mind it well. This is my verra first appearance in your London town, and I'm tellin' you somethin' as from a Scotsman . . . it isnae goin' tae be my last. So mind the name well. When you see it next time, come to the music-hall, and I'll gie you another wee laugh and a sang.'

The management were as happy as Harry. They admitted he was the most successful Scottish act ever to play that theatre, and the best 'extra' turn of the year. They booked him for the rest of that week at a salary of three pounds ten shillings.

Lauder was so elated with his success that he dived into that stocking of sovereigns, and blew the third on drinks all round! That night, as Londoners talked of the funny little Scotsman who had made such a hit at Gatti's-in-the-Road, Harry Lauder from Glasgow slept soundly, a happy smile on his face.

Success, of course, follows success, and as the audiences went out talking about him, so the agents came in to look him over. They arrived in droves, most of them anxious to sign him for future dates. Harry admitted, later in life, that he had been much too impetuous that week. He signed far too many contracts too hurriedly. The agents got him bamboozled. As a result, he got himself tied up too much and committed for work in London theatres at salaries that could easily have been a great deal higher.

Tom Tinsley, naturally, was keen that he should stay on, but he had a previous contract for work at Nottingham, signed months before. Harry had to honour that.

Gatti's-in-the-Road, the free-and-easy hall in the Westminster Bridge Road, where he had made theatrical history for a Scot, was a popular London music-hall. It had opened in 1865, thanks to the enterprise of a caterer named Carlo Gatti. It was the genuine old-style English music-hall, with a table for the chairman, drinks all round, and an open bar at the side of the stalls. But Harry Lauder was to insist, on return visits, that the bar always closed temporarily during his particular act. He wanted – and gained – the full attention of his audience.

The London critics, of course, came in to see the new music-hall 'wonder' from north of the Border, and had to admit he was a merry entertainer. 'A very merry Caledonian', one of them wrote. 'He is certainly something new for London.' And another said: 'This man Harry Lauder brings the scent of the Scottish heather over the footlights into the smoke-laden atmosphere of music-hall.' It was a sentence that Lauder often quoted.

Flushed, but not cocky with his success, Harry Lauder advertised himself to the agents in the theatre trade journals of the day. Here is one of his typical adverts:

HARRY LAUDER
(Eminent Scotch Comedian)
in his Scotch Characters and his famous
CALLIGAN

The Hit of the Season at
GATTI'S, ROAD

Managers, Come and See Me, Call Again.
Monday next, Moss and Stoll Tour

Agent: Cadle, 105 Strand

In another advertisement, Lauder, with a swashbuckling show-manship, told the agents and managers:

'Captured in London'
HARRY LAUDER
Greatest of All Scottish Entertainers has been found guilty of entertaining the audiences of Gatti's, Road and Royal, Holborn last week, sentence being delayed pending enquiries from the principal witnesses Managers of Pavilion, Canterbury, Tivoli, etc.

Counsels for the Defence
Messrs Tom Tinsley and Walter F. Munroe

Lauder also appeared at Gatti's-under-the-Arches, a little music-hall with a tiny stage and only two dressing-rooms. Many stars of the future made early appearances there. The hall was in Villiers Street, in the Strand. He also sang at the Tivoli Theatre, another popular London establishment, and the management immediately reported a great upsurge in attendances.

What exactly was Lauder's trick in catching the smart Londoners and pulling in their applause so strongly? Was there any single secret of his early success? Many asked that question, even in 1900. They still ask it today. Summing up, I'm certain his appeal lay in his freshness and his complete naturalness. He was so different from the rest, all so madly rivalling and copying each other's style. He was a colourful figure in the kilt and wearing his Scottish tam o' shanter. Above all, he was singing them simple songs about ordinary human emotions, and the Londoner, under the skin, was proving himself no different from the fellow up in the North – the man and his wife in the Midlands, on Tyneside or on the Clyde.

Harry Lauder had struck a winning and determined blow for the poor and oft-despised out-of-towners from the country. He had at last made the slick Londoners show a liking for melody and humour from a distant land of mountains and heather. Little did he know that, as the years were to speed by, he was to become a king among international music-hall artistes, Scotland's greatest ambassador in history.

The name 'Harry Lauder' was now high on the billboards in London town. And, as the great English public talked of the laddie from Bonnie Scotland, the songs that he sang began to be heard on everybody's lips. 'Aye, it's a fine thing to sing,' they had told him in his youthful days in the Scottish coal mines. Lauder knew that a singer was very often only as good as the tunes he sang. He made every effort to obtain good ones. Some he wrote himself. Others he created in collaboration with established writers of songs in both London and Glasgow.

Today love songs top the world's hit parades. In Lauder's time a love song wasn't as much of a necessity for a singer as it is today, but it was always a winner if you had a good one in your repertoire.

He was playing London around the winter of 1904 when he

found himself very much in need of a new song. He realised that a good new number would make his act even more popular than it was. Most of all, he was searching for a love lyric that would have its own lilt.

Leaving the theatre one night, he was handed a fan letter by the Cockney stage-doorkeeper. The colourful letter had already attracted attention in the backstage letter-rack. It was in a large pink envelope, with a seal on the back, and the writing was large, sprawly and very feminine. If it had arrived in this modern age, and had been written by a teenager to some celebrated pop-singing idol, it might well have carried the letters S W A L K ('Sealed With A Loving Kiss') on the back of the envelope.

'A letter for you, Mister Lauder, sir,' said the stage-doorkeeper, hardly concealing his curiosity. 'And a very nice one to be sure, Mister 'Arry. It's from a lidy and nobody else, if I'm not mis-taiken.' He coughed, almost apologetically, then: 'I suppose you do love a lassie, sir?'

Harry, smiling broadly, took the pink letter from him, and hurried off into the London fog, shouting back: 'Aye, richt you are, ma mannie. I do love a lassie. And A'm gaun awa' hame tae her the noo!'

Love a lassie! 'I love a lassie'. The words rang in his ears all the way home to his darling Nance in Tooting.

Harry kept the words in his head for several days. He couldn't get them out of his mind, somehow. Maybe this was the new love song he was seeking. Next day he called round to see Gerald Grafton, the well-known London song-writer, and together they worked on the lyric and a melody. Gradually the song took shape. Harry often told how the melody came to him all at once, and he never altered a note afterwards.

Some months later, when the pantomime *Aladdin* opened at the Glasgow Theatre Royal (now a television studio, with more emphasis on electronics, alas, than people) in the Christmas season of 1905, Harry made an instant hit with this new song, singing it for the very first time. The applause on opening night was the talk of Glasgow town.

He was to sing it, as it transpired, many, many times in thousands of towns and cities after that memorable opening night, and he could rarely get off any music-hall or pantomime stage anywhere in the world if he didn't include it in his repertoire. It proved his luckiest and most popular song, bringing him thousands in royalty fees.

Lauder had a happy role in that *Aladdin* of so long ago, for which they paid him the fabulous (for those days) salary of two hundred pounds a week. He played Roderick McSwankey, a young Glasgow lad apprenticed to the Wicked Magician. He also played some scenes with a stage polar bear, and he dressed up as a woman in another scene.

All Glasgow talked about that pantomime as New Year succeeded Christmas, and the year 1906 dawned. And the main talk was about Harry Lauder's success with this catchy new song, *I Love A Lassie*. The city – and much of the rest of Scotland – could talk of little else. 'You must go and see this Harry Lauder as Roderick McSwankey,' was the cry.

The cast was a strong one. Bessie Featherstone played Aladdin, the amusing Dan Crawley was Widow Twankey, and Jose Collins, then a sweet sixteen, was the Second Girl. She went on in later years, incidentally, to shine brightly as a star of musical comedy in America.

Lauder always appreciated how much he owed to this song, *I Love A Lassie*. It caught the public fancy (and soon of a whole nation, as he began to make gramophone records of it) almost overnight, and its fame reached out to all parts of Great Britain.

After that pantomime run, Lauder found himself a national favourite. He was in demand in many theatres, and soon had a date-book that was filled for years ahead. His spare moments – and they were few – were mainly spent after this in looking for another song-hit. He made up his mind he would find a number that would be equally popular. And he did – but in the most unexpected circumstances. He was taking a walk one evening in the summer of 1908 on the road beside the Firth of Clyde, not far from his home of Laudervale, in Dunoon. It was a glorious summer night, just the time for romance.

Ahead of him, in the dusk, Harry spied a pair of young lovers, their arms closely linked together, leisurely roaming along the road towards Innellan. They had their heads close together, and every now and again they would stop, and the boy would kiss his girl. They had thoughts for nothing else in the whole wide world but one another.

The scene stuck in Harry's mind. What could be happier than this kind of roaming in the gloaming, especially by the lovely shores of the Firth of Clyde. It was a romantic scene that was surely being repeated in millions of other places at that very moment – from San Francisco to Johannesburg, from Alaska to Auchtermuchty. If only he could capture the romance of such a scene in song, what a winner he would have!

Harry couldn't wait another minute. He climbed the hill behind Laudervale, looked down on the Firth of Clyde by moonlight, and worked out a verse and chorus. It came to him fairly quickly, and by next evening he had the song complete. But he didn't try it out in public for some time. Instead, he worked on the number constantly, making sure that he had the right introductory script, the most appropriate patter, and the most suitable dress. He thought of nothing else for months and months.

Then, on the opening night of the pantomime *Red Riding Hood*, in the Christmas season of 1910, he launched it on the public. Wisely, Harry chose the same theatre, the Glasgow Theatre Royal in the Cowcaddens district of that city, to introduce it. He had decided to feature it on the same stage which had given him his previous hit, *I Love A Lassie*. The song *Roamin' in the Gloamin'*, had instant acclaim. It was, in fact, an even bigger smash-hit than *I Love A Lassie*, and was to become – though he didn't know it at the time – the number with which he was to be most remembered over the years. Harry used to tell close friends that he rehearsed this song at least five thousand times before using it in public. He often sang himself to sleep at night with it.

Songs were all-important to the Harry Lauder act. He absolutely refused to sing one unless the words came straight from the heart. By today's standards (although, goodness knows, many of the modern hit songs are quite meaningless in their lyrics and quite 'mushy' in their sentiment) a few of Harry Lauder's songs may appear somewhat naive and simple. What we must remember is that they fitted the age and, as dispensed by Lauder, came over the footlights with a homely and natural charm that only Harry himself could add.

He had his favourites among his repertoire of songs, as all great artistes have. Two of his other special loves were *O'er The Hill To Ardentinny* ('Just to see my Bonnie Jeannie') and *My Heather Belle*. He sometimes said that the latter was his 'greatest'. Always a showman, Lauder gave the build-up to his newest songs and, with two great hits already on his hands, he needed to do so. It was hard for him – well-nigh impossible, I may say – to oust the popularity of the first two successes of 1905 and 1910.

And so he kept on singing the songs that his audiences liked best . . . about home, fireside, lochs, moors and mountains, bonnie lassies and love-sick laddies. He gave his theatre audiences more Sandys and Jeannies and Maggies and Bellas and Lachies and

Jocks than the world had ever known. But nobody complained about their popularity.

About this time, a twelve-year-old lad from Liverpool, a former newspaper seller and lather-boy in a barber's shop, started work at Liverpool's Empire Theatre as call-boy.

William Chidlo, 'Chirpy' as he became known, recalls the first occasion Harry Lauder topped the bill at the Empire.

It was an eight-act bill that week. The Four Astors opened the show with a song-and-dance act, and then came a couple of crosstalk comedians. Lily Langtry, the well-known comedienne, was the third act, to be followed by a juggling turn, and then by the Two Black Crows, two coloured gentlemen in full evening dress, at the piano.

But the act everyone went to see was Harry Lauder's. It was obviously the big moment of the night, and the audience showed it by their expectant hush as they waited for his entrance. Chirpy couldn't resist peeping from the wings after he had given Mr Lauder his cue.

'The applause was terrific, the encores were deafening,' he says. 'Oh, boy, Harry Lauder got them as soon as he went out there. And he kept them there – right in the palm of his hand.

'It was excitement all the way. The full-house boards were out, and the front-of-the-house uniform men were shouting "Standing Room Only". Harry really gave them the works, and at each house took several curtain calls. With a swirl and tilt of his kilt, he would thrust his knobbly bent stick out towards the audience with a Scottish hooch, and then he'd slowly leave the stage, mopping his brow.'

Chirpy remembers the Lauder routine well, as any impressionable theatre call-boy must. Slowly, the great little minstrel would make his way down to his dressing-room, the perspiration running down his cheeks. Then he would flop into a chair, throw off his shoes, take off his tam-o'-shanter bonnet, discard his jacket and sporran, and drink a bottle of stout. Then he would fill his pipe slowly and just sit there, puffing steadily and relaxing. He had the happy knack of being able to forget the stage completely between acts.

A little later, Lauder would put on his trousers and jacket, and take his mackintosh, and slip quietly out of the theatre into the pub next door, the *Leggs of Man*. Or he might walk over to the other end of Lime Street to the well-known and popular *Wine Lodge* where all the professional acts from the many music-halls around the Mersey used to meet.

This haunt of the English vaudevillians was up the stairs, brass plates protecting each step, and with a dimly-lit interior. It was a small but really comfortable, cosy Victorian bar. The lady manageress was a tall, good-looking woman, her face well-painted, and with a bustle to her rustling silk black dress. She knew personally all the artistes, and had made a stab herself at the music-hall in her day.

The walls of that bar were covered with photographs of English music-hall artistes and of American performers who had played England. But pride of place went to one man – Harry Lauder.

That *Wine Lodge* is no longer there. The building and all the others on the site have been demolished to make way for a new high-storey building. What wonderful and warm music-hall memories disappeared with it!

Harry Lauder always had a soft spot in his Scottish heart for Liverpool and the Merseyside region of England. It was partly because of the warm reception the audiences gave him, and partly because of his close link with the dear old Argyle Theatre in Birkenhead, which had given him an early chance when few wanted to know him.

Chirpy Chidlo remembers Harry Lauder as 'a very rich man

who talked lovingly about his younger brothers'. He recalls: 'He was a lovable character with his chubby face, plump nose, twinkling eyes, and bushy eyebrows. He wasn't a bit brash or boastful. He kept his talk, voice and talent for the stage and his audiences.

'Without his Scottish regalia, you would never have thought he was a professional artiste. He was a master of make-up. I knew I wanted to go on the music-halls myself, and I stood with wide-eyed wonderment when Lauder applied his stage make-up. He did it from foundation to finish in a flash.

'Oh, boy, what that man could do with a few greasepaints, pencils and a powder puff! He knew it all. It was a work of art, and quite professional. I stood on a chair and helped him into his well-worn, two-toned coloured woollen dressing-gown.'

One night young Chidlo made bold to ask the great man a question.

'Mister Lauder,' he began, 'could you please tell me something? Who writes and composes these many moving Scottish songs with the lilting melodies?'

Harry looked back at him with a roguish smile and replied, with a cheery wink: 'A Scotsman, laddie . . . a Scot . . . a man by the name o' – Harry Lauder!'

When young Chidlo told Lauder he hoped to be going on the music-halls himself later in life, the star smiled and gave him happy encouragement.

'Aye, you couldn't do better,' he told him. 'You're just the braw laddie for the job.'

One evening the call-boy asked Lauder why he wore a neat, small, lightweight racehorse shoe. Harry looked a bit surprised, for it was probably a secret. As it was covered with white heather, the youngster again asked the reason.

'Weel, it's my secret,' replied Lauder. 'But I'll tell you. You see, we Scottish Highlanders believe that white heather brings us luck and protects us from danger.'

Chirpy's last memory of Harry Lauder was as he shook his knobbly bent stick towards him and said: 'You know, laddie, I've got many sticks, but I like this particular-r-r one the best. Why? Because it's got knobs on . . .'

Once, during his appearance in Liverpool, Lauder called the young page-boy into his dressing-room and adopted a most serious look.

'Chirpy,' he asked, 'did you ever know of a Scotsman who gave away a five-shilling piece instead of a tanner [a sixpence]?'

'No, I never did,' said Chirpy, wondering what revelation was coming next. (Lauder had a great dramatic sense and could keep all his listeners poised on every word.)

The Scot paused for effect and replied: 'Well, laddie, neither did I!' And he chuckled merrily to himself.

'But he did, once, give me a silver five-shilling piece,' Chirpy remembers. 'He was quite a generous man, despite the image. As he gave it to me, he looked at me, real serious, and said: "Do you know, laddie, that is what I was paid for my verra first paid singing engagement – five shillings".'

Before they parted, Lauder handed Chirpy a rough, black-and-white sketch which he had drawn of the pair of them together. It was autographed: 'Yours Sincerely, Harry Lauder'.

For months and years afterwards, Chirpy Chidlo, who by now had joined his first song-and-dance act, watched the theatrical calls in the showbusiness weeklies. He hoped that, when he went out on tour, he might appear on a bill with the great Harry Lauder.

But he had no such luck. Lauder was always one or two weeks ahead of him at various theatres. Chirpy still watched the calls faithfully – until Lauder himself made his own last call and took his final curtain.

The call-boy and the star he so much admired never met again.

The Thrifty Scot

Was Harry Lauder really a mean man? Or did he make a big pretence of being regarded as mean – for the sake of the publicity it would bring him? Many have argued out that question, and remained quite unaware of the true situation.

He certainly created and built-up the image of a miserly, skinflint Scot, assiduously counting the pennies and cents, and stacking them away for the joyful purpose of simply amassing wealth. The world, enjoying the picture to the full, took up this image and built it along with Lauder.

His kilt, his tartan, his tam-o'-shanter bonnet, his knobbly sticks were, of course, sufficient gimmick in themselves. But he had this don't-spend-a-cent gimmick as well. It became famous all round the globe. Most of all, it tickled the fancy of millions of Americans, poor as well as rich.

Harry Lauder certainly propagated the 'mean Scot' jokes. Through him, in fact, has arisen the picture that still exists today of canny, ultra-thrifty, sometimes skinflint Scotsmen.

The rumour spread in the showbusiness of his time that Harry Lauder would never buy anyone a drink. Stage-doorkeepers talked of it. Fellow-artistes passed it on. True? Or false? The latter assumption must be correct. Harry Lauder spread this story himself. And hundreds more. In an expansive mood, he once laughed and told me: 'I've always been a one to set these Harry Lauder jokes on the go. In fact, man, I'm a joke propagator. My friend, Henry Ford, got the idea of a joke factory, and he actually wanted me to run it for him! What a great and wonderful idea! Aye, an' I'd have been the ideal chap, I'm tellin' you.

'Mind you, though, I'm tellin' you, these Harry Lauder jokes have made an awful lot o' people happy. Even when they've come back to me after going all round the world, I've started more fresh yins o' my own – a' aboot myself and my own meanness.'

Lauder was happy to let the 'meanness' gimmick snowball, and roll ahead of him as one of the greatest free-publicity tricks of all time.

Jack Benny – his fellow-Americans gag about *his* meanness! – can hardly be compared with a master of the image-building like Lauder. Jack admitted this to me when we talked about Harry in his dressing-room at the old Empire Theatre in Glasgow some years ago. 'A master of the art of creating a gimmick', was how he described him.

Lauder's 'thrifty Scotsman' jokes were simple and straightforward. But my, how the smart show-going set in America loved them! And repeated them. He used to joke that he always filled his pen when he called at his bank to arrange about an overdraft. Why? Because, as he chuckled, 'it's better-quality ink than whit you get at the post office!'

One of his favourite stories was about 'two men frae Glasgow. They set oot in a rowing boat for the Black Sea – they wanted tae fill their fountain pens. Aye, there's enterprise for ye, man!'

Another Lauder story concerned a Scotsman who was waiting for St Peter's permission to enter the Golden Gates. He was asked what he had done in life, and he told them. They checked back on his records. Then St Peter asked his nationality.

'I'm a Scotsman,' he said. St Peter scratched his head and looked doubtful.

'I don't know if we can make porridge just for one,' he said.

'But, tell you what, I'll go and see.'

When St Peter came back, the Scotsman had gone [*dramatic pause here by Sir Harry*] – 'but so had the Golden Gates!'

Bennett Cerf, in his book *Shake Well Before Using*[1], tells the story of Harry Lauder's American secretary. She had a young daughter and, after ignoring a number of pointed hints, the Scots comedian finally gave her a pass for one of his matinées in New York.

'Orchestra seats!' exclaimed the secretary. 'How wonderful!' Then she added, sadly: 'But my little girl hasn't got a dress that's pretty enough for the orchestra!'

'Ah, weel, we'll soon remedy that,' replied Sir Harry. And he tore up the pass for the orchestra seats and made out a new one for two – in the second balcony!

Doubtless, that one also started with a man called Lauder!

If you examine the Lauder stage act, and the patter he used, you'll find that, next to love and bonnie lassies, the subject he talked about most was money. He used to tell of the wee Aberdeen man who was walking down Union Street in his native city. Alongside him walked the only Jew who ever succeeded in earning a living in Scotland's Granite City of the north-east. Suddenly the Jew bent down and picked up half a crown from the pavement in front of the Aberdonian's feet. The shrewd little Aberdeen man said nothing. But, inside thirty seconds, he asked politely to be excused, and rushed off down the street.

Where to? As Lauder explained, he was off to the nearest opticians' to have his eyesight tested. He just couldn't afford to make the same mistake twice!

Harry couldn't resist a joke which pin-pointed this alleged ultra-thrifty and canny streak in the Scot. Even when it concerned a child. He told of a wee Scots lad in London who wrote home

[1] *Shake Well Before Using*, Bennett Cerf, Hammond, Hammond, 1956

to his mother in Auchtermuchty, Fife: 'This is a gr-r-reat big town and the restaurants are just gr-r-rand. Ye see, A'm always findin' a threepenny piece hidden underneath my plate as a surprise!'

Harry Lauder had a favourite practical joke which he often used in public. It was his own invention, too, embellished somewhat after a huddle with his business manager, Tom Vallance. They would choose a conspicuous settee in a crowded hotel lounge. Then Lauder would send a page-boy out for two penny newspapers, handing him a threepenny piece.

The boy would dash off, come back and hand over the papers and expect, naturally, that Sir Harry would allow him to keep the change. So the page-boy would walk away, clutching the coin. Harry always let the boy get half-way across the hotel lounge floor. Then, in a very loud Scottish voice, he would yell: 'Hey, boy. Come back here, boy!'

When the boy was a dozen yards away, Sir Harry would yell: 'Whit aboot ma penny change? I gave ye thruppence, laddie, r-r-remember-r-r!'

The trick never failed. Everyone in that hotel lounge stopped talking. The poor page-boy would blush deep-red. And another story of the Lauder 'meanness' would go round and round, and far beyond the walls of that hotel. Those who knew the gag loved to see it in operation.

What Sir Harry didn't tell anybody – and very few people ever knew – was that the victims of these practical jokes were later given a very handsome tip by the crafty wee Scot.

Lauder, in public, didn't tip. Many blamed him for it. But they would have praised him had they known that he always handed out his gratuities in secret, when nobody was looking. It would have destroyed his wonderful image build-up if he had been spotted being generous.

Stage-doorkeepers in the theatre are shrewd judges of character, and can tell you many a story of theatrical meanness, even in this modern age. When Harry Lauder played a long season at the Palace Theatre in London's Shaftesbury Avenue, he got lots of help from the stage-doorkeeper. Then the run came to an end, and the final night arrived. As he left the theatre, Lauder halted at the stage-door, and handed the doorman his parting tip. It was – a signed picture-postcard of himself!

The profession talked for months about his meanness after that well-publicised incident. So did the public. What the world never realised was that this particular stage-doorkeeper was in alliance with Harry over the trick, and had been previously rewarded with a quite generous farewell gratuity.

The Harry Lauder stories did the little minstrel more good, publicity-wise, than all the Press coverage he received, great as that was. He called these stories 'the verra finest free advertisement any stage performer could have hoped for'. People, half-believing them, would re-tell these 'mean' jokes time and again. They went round and round the world. They preceded him on his long trips across the United States. New jokes were even dreamed up by total strangers, and little bits were added on to the original ones to give them a new twist.

He once gave a tip of twopence to a porter at Queen Street Station, in Glasgow. A close friend meeting him saw this, and suggested it was the wrong thing to do, especially in his home town. 'No' one bit,' said Lauder. 'I know that porter fine. The last time I was here, I gave him a shilling, and he was quite nasty about the size o' the tip. Now that he's got only tuppence, he'll spread the story like wildfire, and my name will be on everybody's lips this week.'

Once, at Glasgow Empire, a friend gave him three cigars as a present. Next morning Lauder went to a tobacconist and exchanged the cigars for two ounces of his favourite roll of tobacco. He smoked nothing else, and he wasn't going to waste the precious cigars!

Privately, he was a generous man, quite removed from the image he cultivated. In his hotel bedroom one day a friend found him with a bunch of letters and envelopes spread out before him. They were from people down on their luck, all genuine cases. Harry was busy putting ten-shilling and one-pound notes into them; into one he was inserting a five-pound note.

Money, thought of purely as money, meant very little to Harry Lauder all his life, for his wants were small. Mind you, he liked money for the security it brought him. He used to say that a man got a 'cosy feeling' when he had sufficient in the bank for all that might happen in life. He believed, too, that he was as entitled to all the money he earned (and he earned plenty in days when income tax was much less demanding) as were all the show-business managers and theatre proprietors who had made thousands of dollars off him while paying him a one-hundredth part of the total.

But money, in itself, didn't make Harry Lauder happy. What did give him pleasure was 'the fighting for it'. 'It's knowing,' he used to say, 'that white, black, brown and yellow men have been willing to pay it out just to hear me and see me and cheer me.'

Nevertheless, true Scot that he was, Lauder hated anyone to 'sting' him. Once, travelling through Euston Station, in London on the way home to Clydeside, he gave a railway porter his luggage and made the awful mistake of handing him the wrong tip. He gave him a golden sovereign in mistake for a silver shilling. When Harry found out, two minutes later, he let out a yell, and went running after him. But the porter wasn't to be seen.

Next morning, when he reached Scotland, he found that his best golf-bag was missing. Generously but sadly, he commented:

'I bet that porter was so overcome with his tip he forgot to put the bag in with the rest of the luggage.'

But the great wee Scots entertainer had to go short of his 'baps and bannocks' for a long time after that. He hadn't yet reached the stage of being wealthy enough not to miss a single golden sovereign.

All through his career he kept up the 'canny Scotsman' stories. He used to gag: 'I'm so mean that, tae save ma handkerchiefs, I just go to the door an' let the wind blow ma nose!' Or, again: 'I'm left-handed, so I keep ma money in the right-hand jacket pocket!'

But the story Lauder loved most was about the Scotsman, the Englishman and the Welshman, all in a pub enjoying a pint. Then a great big bluebottle fell into each of their pints. The Englishman flicked his out. The Welshman blew his out. But the canny wee Scotsman – he *wrung* his out!

At the end of one fabulously successful tour of America, Harry surprised everybody by arranging to hold a grand party at his hotel – for thirty special people, and no more!

Solemnly, he told his guests: 'But remember-r-r-r, folks, you can stay here for only two hour-r-rs!'

Hearing this, and taking the Scot seriously, the maître d'hôtel whispered to Harry; 'But really . . . there's no extra charge if your guests stay a bit later, Mr Lauder!'

Whereupon Lauder further nonplussed the company: 'Och, aye, you can stay as long as you like, folks. I'd also invite you a' tae the theatre, only I'm no playin' there masel this week.

'An' whit's more, I've spent so much damn money on this food here, I havena' ony dollars left tae buy your theatre tickets!'

'Thy People Shall Be My People'

AMERICA AND ITS entertainment market has been tackled by many British and European theatre artistes in recent years, but the going is always tough. It is not easy for a Britisher or a Frenchman or a German to adjust a song or comedy act to a great new audience in a different continent, cosmopolitan though that audience may be. Many have tried to 'conquer' America as entertainers, and found it impossible.

Young Harry Lauder, I know, had similar doubts when the name 'America' was first suggested to him. But he remembered that many Scots before him had set out to make their fame and fortune in other lands, and to be pioneers. He saw no reason why he himself shouldn't at least have a stab, just as he had tackled the big city of London. Lauder had sometimes thought of crossing to the United States for a vacation. It would at least give him a peep at this great New World so many were talking about.

One day Harry's agent in London, George Foster, told him he had received an offer of a five-weeks' run in New York.

'It's maybe just what you're needing at this stage,' said George. 'A new outlet for your act. An awful lot of people live in America, Harry, my lad. And a lot of them are from Scotland, too. Besides, it will give you a bit of a holiday as well.'

At first Harry said he wasn't interested, as, indeed, he wasn't. He was getting plenty of work in the music-halls of England. But, for a laugh, he quoted a sum which he fondly imagined would put off all further inquiries.

George Foster sent off a cable to New York quoting the terms on which the little Scots comedian would be available. At that particular moment Lauder was appearing at Liverpool, in north-west England, and earning about twenty pounds for a week's work.

The New York agent considered the offer, and sent back his reply. To Lauder's complete surprise, he accepted. It was a fantastic offer, the kind of money wee Harry had never even dreamed of getting.

He dashed into the nearest post office in Liverpool, and sent off a telegram to his wife at their home in Tooting, in London, detailing the offer, and asking: 'Will you come with me if this deal gets through?'

The reply that Nance sent back to Harry must be unique, almost a classic, in the annals of showbusiness. It said, simply: 'SEE BOOK OF RUTH CHAPTER ONE VERSE SIXTEEN LOVE, NANCE'.

Harry was intrigued – but not surprised. Both he and Nance were deeply religious people, and often read the Bible in the evening together. Hurriedly, with some excitement, Harry searched his cheap Liverpool lodgings for a copy of the Bible, and turned up the Book of Ruth. And there, in Verse Sixteen of Chapter One, he read:

> And Ruth said, Intreat me not to leave thee, or to return from following after thee; for whither thou goest, I will go; and where thou lodgest, I will lodge; thy people shall be my people, and thy God my God.

Harry needed no further thought. His darling wife Nancy was ready and happy to tackle America with him. She had given him the best tonic of the day in this novel reply to his telegram.

So, on a dull and wet October morning in 1907, with ships'

sirens blaring through the messy mist of Merseyside, the liner *Lucania* slipped out into the Irish Sea and the broad Atlantic, bound for New York. At the last moment Nancy had found herself unable to make the journey because of family ties, but she suggested that son John should go in her place and help keep an eye on his father in America.

Thus it came about that two of the happiest but most anxious passengers aboard the *Lucania* that winter's morning were a Mr Harry Lauder, from Bonnie Scotland, and his son John, then a schoolboy of fourteen.

Harry's nervousness at the unknown scene ahead of him increased considerably in mid-Atlantic when he came across an old New York newspaper in the ship's lounge. There, in bold type was a mention of himself. A writer called Alan Dale was discussing his act and criticising his physical appearance, his bandy legs, his voice, and his brashness in thinking he could appeal to Americans. It added the final touch by naming him as 'this Scotch buffoon who has the insolence to call himself a comedian'.

Poor Harry was worried sick by that article. He fretted over it and became angry. 'Tell me, John, what dae you make o' it?' he asked his son.

The lad laughed heartily at the article. 'Don't worry one wee bit, Pa,' he said. 'This is the funniest thing I've read about you yet. It makes you out such a comic everybody will want to see you now.'

But Harry Lauder still worried, even when the *Lucania* slipped into New York Harbour and a swarm of eager-beaver New York newspapermen came rushing aboard to interview the odd-looking celebrity from the British music-hall world and the backwoods of Bonnie Scotland.

Harry's manner was slightly arrogant and aggrieved, and he wasn't on his best behaviour with the New York Press. 'Tell me,' he demanded, 'What one o' you is Alan Dale? I'm dyin' tae get these hands on him!'

The New York reporters looked puzzled. 'Alan Dale?' they repeated. 'Never heard of him. We did see something he wrote about you, but we don't know the guy. He's not one of the regular crowd.'

But still Harry Lauder refused to be appeased. He was far from being his usual expansive and affable self in his interview, and clearly got the wrong side of the Press men who had come aboard to meet him.

'Say, Mister Scottie, don't be such a sour little guy!' one of them bluntly told him. 'Quit the fightin' talk, Mister Lauder,' said another. 'We ain't come here to do battle, just to get your story.'

The Klaw and Erlanger variety agency had sent down two representatives from their New York office to greet the little Scot. They stood quietly in the background, nervously biting their fingers as Harry crossed swords with the powerful New York Press. Then they returned to their office and reported.

'Say, boss,' said one, 'this li'l guy Lauder takes the cake. He's here all right, in person, all decked out, but what a fuss he's causing! He's shoutin' at the pier porters and playin' merry hell with the newspaper fellows. Says he'll show us what a Scotsman can do on the stage.

'He's four foot an' no more in height, has thick rimless eye-glasses, and looks a real country bumpkin in a shabby old tartan coat and baggy pants. He'll flop for us, boss, an' that's no kiddin'. Why don't we ship him right back to the heather where he comes from?'

The shipboard argument aside, however, Harry Lauder was given a warm welcome from Scots friends on the pier. His old friend Peter Dewar, the whisky man, was there, and had laid on a group of Highland pipers in full Scottish regalia to pipe him ashore and lead the way to a tartan-decked automobile. Lauder and his son drove thus in state to the Knickerbocker Hotel that Friday evening, with the heads of curious New Yorkers turning to stare, and went early to bed.

It was a busy weekend. On the following morning Harry and John were out early, gazing at the wonderful sights all around them. Similarly, the passing New Yorkers gazed in wonder at the little kilted figure and his teenage son, and were equally intrigued, especially by the kilt.

Harry was billed to open at the matinée performance on the Monday. It was at the New York Theatre in Times Square. Father and son turned up an hour before the show, and nervously prepared for the reception in this strange and madly modern city three thousand miles across the sea from Glasgow and the Clyde.

Would he take a trick with his simple Scottish act? Or would he fail miserably in this slick and sophisticated city of rush and bustle where, maybe, simple homely things didn't mean so much? Lauder wondered as he waited nervously in the wings.

Then he was on, the songs about Scotland were echoing through the theatre, and – surprise, surprise – the tough New Yorkers were actually cheering and applauding vigorously. His entrance alone had been the signal for a wave of cheers and 'Guid Luck, Harry!' cries from exiled Scots in the audience. Lauder said later that he had been on that stage only sixty seconds when he instinctively got the feeling he was going to 'click' and register. Then he sang *Tobermory*, and the customers went wild with delight. Here was a little man from Bonnie Scotland with magic in his music.

Harry afterwards confessed to me that this was one of the great and magic moments in his own life. He knew from that moment on that he was going to love America, just as America was destined to love Lauder. At the matinée performance he had to sing six songs in place of the three he had planned. In the evening the patrons cheered so much he had to give them ten numbers before he was even allowed to leave the stage.

Next morning John Lauder got up early, dashed out of the Knickerbocker Hotel and bought up all the main New York newspapers. Returning to the hotel, he awoke his father and read him the notices of the critics. It was praise . . . praise . . . praise all the way. The name Lauder was prominent in all the headlines. One particularly caught the attention:

HARRY LAUDER, GREAT ARTIST, CAPTIVATES AMERICA!

If you look back through the files of *Variety*, you find, in the issue of the 9th November 1907 a very full account, written by the founder of the newspaper, Sime Silverman, of Harry Lauder's act on this, his début on the American stage.

Here, in part, is what Sime said of Harry Lauder and his sixty-three minutes' act of character songs that November of 1907:

> Oh, yon Harry Lauder! And after which remark, you must come to a full stop. That will express as well as columns the impression the great Scotch singing character comedian left on the audience at the New York Theatre last Monday night, his second appearance on an American stage.
>
> Lauder is distinct, unique, and a revelation in vaudeville. His Scotch dialect is broad at times, but it is not always necessary that he be heard to be understood.
>
> For twenty-four minutes Mr Lauder stood before the footlights as a woe-begone youngster, looking over the mutilated toys removed from several pockets, and had he not uttered a syllable the applause would have been exactly as voluminous. The twenty-four minutes seemed like ten. This is his best characterisation, or at least it was that on Monday evening.
>
> Mr Lauder is a master of facial expression. While detailing his experiences in the garb of a youngster, he recited the meeting with

76

an old man, and instanter he would become the old man in a fleeting change of expression, reverting to the childish character the next moment.

It is nothing short of remarkable character acting, really wonderful, something vaudeville has never seen before, nor the legitimate for that matter, either. While as a boy Mr Lauder sang *The Saftest Of The Family*, giving a juvenile monologue after the second verse. For the opening, the Scotchman 'did' a 'party gathering' (where different persons were called upon), concluding with *Stop Your Tickling, Jock!*, or *My Scotch Blue Bell* was rendered.

For the finale a pretty blonde girl came stealing upon the stage, and was introduced as 'That's Her', his 'Blue Bell'. The audience believed just what Mr Lauder said. He is never 'on the stage' during the act. The man's personality is so potent that you feel he is with you or you with him. The footlights do not interfere.

After a speech and tumultuous applause, Mr Lauder sang *We Parted On The Shore*, dressed as a sailor who had never been to sea, a crystal-clear comedy creation. Another speech informed the big gathering that he thought just enough had been given.

Monday night brought out that this foreigner is a facile speechmaker; an easy extem speaker, perfectly self-possessed. It also made plain that he has been widely copied over here, both in actions and jokes.

A typical Scotch slang phrase is probably 'Bung up in the brew', which Mr Lauder used to express how he had struck the other fellow. *She's My Daisy*, a song made famous abroad by the comedian, was not heard, although expected, but he must have a vast repertoire stored away.

Then the reviewer Sime, after this high praise for the act, summed up the Scot in what, that November of 1907, were to be prophetic words so far as American audiences and Harry Lauder were concerned.

'Harry Lauder is booked to remain in New York for five weeks,' he wrote. 'He could remain six months. An ovation never equalled on the variety platform was his reception.

'The house was crowded by his countrymen, but you do not have to wear kilts to appreciate him. A single act to occupy over an hour without tiring! There is no answer. He elevates vaudeville, and could do the same to the legitimate. Art is symbolic of Harry Lauder, the greatest of them all.'

'The Scotchman', this facile, personality-packed 'foreigner', as *Variety* had described him, was to return many times over the years to the United States of America, playing to sell-out business in theatres and earning more money than any other visiting European had ever pulled in. He was to play, first, for 2,500 dollars a week, and then for 3,000 dollars a week. His agent, William Morris, was to buy out his prior contracts with managers across in England by paying them as much as 1,000 dollars a week for Lauder's release.

As his fame and name increased in stature, he was to find his salary shooting up to between 4,000 and 5,000 dollars a week over many, many years. One American tour, lasting for nearly a year, was to bring him in a total of 120,000 dollars. He was earning well over 4,500 dollars a week in the good old days when income-tax demands were so much less and money really meant something in value.

That November 1907 date at the New York Theatre in Times Square started the avalanche. Bookings poured in on him. When he played the Lincoln Square Theatre in October of the following year, 1908, he did a seventy-minutes' act and garnered an even warmer reception. One night he held the stage, alone, for an hour and fifteen minutes. Great enthusiasm swept over the huge audience when the little Scot came on the stage. So great was the din that he had to be speechless at several points during his act, unable to make himself heard.

For his October 1908 visit Harry Lauder took over to America a budget of new songs, but despite this, the old ones held their

78

established place. One that took a really big trick, oddly enough, was the typically Scottish *I'm The Saftest O' The Family*, which one reviewer described as 'by long odds the best of the lot'.

Lauder's twist of humour into pathos registered strongly with the Americans, a sentimental race despite their outward sharpness. They also loved his lilting *The Wedding Bells Were Ringing*, and his character study of a Scot who had over-imbibed at a wedding reception.

His act at the Lincoln Square Theatre included the lightsome number *When I Get Back To Bonnie Scotland*, always a firm favourite with the Americans, *Wedding Bells*, *I Love A Lassie*, and *We Parted On The Shore*. Towards the end of the act members of the audience became a bit unruly in their demands for more, and there were many shouts of 'Give us another song, Harry' and loud cries for the number *She's Ma Daisy*.

The act, on the whole, was voted 'an even greater success' than that of his first visit the previous year, although that initial success must have been hard, indeed, to better.

The years from 1907 onwards were the golden years for Harry Lauder. America, land of the almighty dollar, gave him the welcome mat, and beckoned him back across the Atlantic time and again.

Little did he realise, when he made that first nervous trip in the winter of 1907, that it was to be the first of many. In fact, he was to make twenty-two trips in all to North America, each one more successful than the last. It is no wonder that the people of the United States speak his name almost in reverence today.

These trips set the seal on his fame and fortune. They brought him so much money that he came to win a unique place in show-business for a very down-to-earth reason. He earned so much that he could retire to live in comfort and luxury after a comparatively brief career.

The present-day star keeps going the rounds, and not always because he loves the business! In many instances it is a case of necessity; he has to stay before the bright lights in order to pay his rent and keep his family in days when super-tax takes so large a whack of a salary.

In 1908, on his second tour, Harry Lauder's salary had sky-rocketed to 5,000 dollars a week. Theatre managements in Boston, Chicago, Pittsburgh, Philadelphia and New York City were happy to pay out that kind of money, and even more if he had asked for it. Harry spent ten weeks of that fourteen-weeks' tour in New York. The rest were out-of-town dates.

By 1911 the tour had stretched to last all of six months. Now he was getting 1,000 dollars a night, with all expenses paid. He was, in fact, earning more money than any other single star in the world. What a triumph for the once poor miner lad! These were the great days of vaudeville. It was the era of the Ziegfeld Follies, of the Dolly Sisters and Fanny Brice (with her dying swan burlesque), of Leon Errol and Bert Williams, the song-and-dance comedian. Billie Burke was starring in the legitimate theatre, and the big names in vaudeville were Gallagher and Shean, Vesta Victoria and Blossom Seeley.

But the Harry Lauder name shone as brightly as anyone. His publicity preceded him in every town and city, and 'Harry Lauder stories', as they came to be known, were told and retold, everywhere. An American had only to remark on 'that li'l Skatch guy in the kilt', and it was a cue for another gag or joke about Scotch meanness.

The United States was a lively and prosperous land. People thronged to the vaudeville shows, and if the name Harry Lauder was on the billboards, they went all the faster. He was the kind of draw you get only once or twice in a half-century in the live theatre. Harry was now meeting up with the great ones of the nation. He was playing golf with President Taft and other notables. The wealthy and important ones of America were waiting to shake his hand.

It was strenuous work, this touring of so vast a country. The procedure in the daily routine could so easily become monotonous. Harry and his entourage were up at six each morning, and usually caught their train at seven. Breakfast was a hurried coffee and a couple of sandwiches at a railside depot. They didn't get to their destination until around six in the evening. A journey of 450 miles took that time. Tea was a couple of boiled eggs and a slice of bread.

At seven Harry would be met by the local Caledonian Society. There was the warm welcome from Scottish exiles, and then the theatre show, lasting from eight until probably eleven-fifteen. Supper, to bed, and then off again next day, arriving this time for lunch at 12.45, and taking apple-pie and coffee with the office-bearers of the next Caledonian Society. Often, a matinée show was scheduled from 2 pm to 4.15 pm.

Then it was off again at, say, 5 pm, to catch a train for Milwaukee, eighty miles away. An evening theatre show, and then the same procedure all over again as the coast-to-coast trek continued.

Harry Lauder thrived on it. The Americans loved his amazing energy and thrilled to know that he was coming right to their own city or town. The local Scots colony – and it was usually a considerable one – made it the tartan night of the year.

His American agent, William Morris, who became a personal friend of the Lauder clan, arranged all Harry's tours of the States, and the schedulings were often complex and considerable. Once, after spending some weeks in New York playing to excellent business, Harry and his wife practically lived on a train for six months. He used to chuckle in later years when, adding up all the weeks of American travel, he would suddenly discover that he had spent several years of his life on American trains.

'The Harry Lauder Specials' were glamorous and luxurious for the era. Normally, they were made up of three coaches – a baggage car, a Pullman sleeping-car for the company, and a parlour-car for Harry, Nance, and agent Bill Morris. In the early years of touring Lauder was even given the use of the famous Riva saloon which Theodore Roosevelt used during his Presidential journeyings; he was thrilled to learn that Sarah Bernhardt had travelled in the same train before him.

The trains were routed, without necessity for change, right across the United States. Lauder travelled many thousands of miles in them, and was involved only once in an accident when another train collided with his at Buffalo. Although considerable damage was caused, Lauder was fortunate to escape without injury.

San Francisco was a favourite city of Harry Lauder. He always received a warm welcome there, and sometimes made it a jumping-off ground for trips across to Australia and New Zealand. He usually returned to Britain this way. Chicago, too, he liked and there were many fans in Detroit, Boston and Philadelphia.

When time permitted, Harry made a trip down into Mexico and was fascinated by the people, just as they were themselves by the Great Scot.

His visits to California were, of course, always interesting. Harry liked the silent cinema, and he loved to wander through the early studios, meeting up with his friend Charlie Chaplin and Charlie's brother, Syd, in Hollywood. Chaplin said that Lauder was one of his favourite friends.

The members of Scottish societies supported Lauder at his concerts all across America. Some even arrived at the theatres carrying their bagpipes with them! Others wore Balmoral bonnets and jackets of tartan. Their patriotism and nostalgia knew few bounds. A Scot abroad is even more Scottish than a Scot at home.

Once, backstage in a New York theatre, Harry was handed a note from a man in the audience. He wrote on it that he was a Scots exile living in the Klondyke, and that he had a personal message from five hundred miners up there, many of them from Scotland. They had heard of Lauder's appearance in New York, and had run a sweepstake in connection with it. The winner was this visitor to New York, given instructions to meet Harry backstage, obtain the words of all his songs, and take back a signed photograph of the minstrel to prove he had actually met him. It had taken the tough Scot from the Klondyke all of two weeks to make the journey.

Harry Lauder, elated but surprised that anyone should attempt such a long trip, welcomed the Scotsman to his dressing-room, gave him the required song information, and suggested he stay on for another two evenings. He was thrilled when he was given a seat in the wings during one of the shows. Two days later he set off again for the Klondyke, the happiest traveller out of New York. He was a man from Ayrshire, and he never forgot that trip of a lifetime.

Wherever he moved in the United States, Lauder found the people fascinating as well as friendly. He was constantly surprised by how different they were from state to state and city to city.

Any man who makes over twenty trips to the same country is certain to get to know its people well. Harry Lauder made the most of every visit. He went to see round all the historical places, was shown over factories, and often went as a guest to the Rotary Club meetings in each town or city.

In Salt Lake City he met members of the Mormon community and admired the extremely efficient manner in which the affairs of the city were conducted.

Washington, DC, Chicago, Denver, Montana, Illinois . . . name any American city, town or state, and Lauder had played it. He loved them all, and the Americans loved him, making him a Freeman in many a place he visited. The friendliness of Americans appealed greatly to his warm heart, but he never singled them out from other nations. Harry Lauder often said that, no matter where you went in the world, people were 'the same under the surface'.

'Aye,' he'd remark, in that honest Scottish burr, 'I'm tellin' you, lad. They're a' looking for a wee bit o' fellowship and laughter rather than hatred and sorrow.

'If, by bein' a simple Scots comic, and singin' bonnie humorous songs, I can do my wee bit to help make the world a brighter place, and help mysel' along the road at the same time, well, then, I'm richt glad to lend a hand.'

He was an international ambassador who had no axe to grind – except to make the world a happier place for everyone, no matter the colour of their skin.

Gradually, over the years, and thanks to his constant tours, Harry Lauder built up for himself a name that spelt out magic with audiences all over the United States of America. As the early years of this century passed, he created for himself a following second to none for an artiste from Europe.

This was obvious in the early winter of 1911 when the Scot made yet another visit to New York. As one observer pointed out, the proceedings attending the début of Lauder's 1911 show at the Manhattan Opera House were 'undoubtedly without precedent in American theatrical history'.

He was crossing this time from Britain in the liner *Saxonia*, but its arrival in New York was delayed by storms out in mid-Atlantic. He was due to open at the matinée show on the Monday, but when it became obvious that the liner would not dock until late that same evening, the matinée was abandoned.

William Morris, Harry's agent, knew there would be gaps to fill, and that the audience would have a long wait until the kilted Scot could make his appearance. So he sent out an S O S to various top supporting artistes in New York and gathered them at the theatre to fill the bill.

It was to become one of the most frantic and breathtaking 'rescue' efforts of the New York vaudeville world. The Harry Lauder Show, as planned by the management of the Opera House, was to have been composed of five acts, in addition to the star. But, on that historic Monday night, more than twenty acts appeared on the stage in one of its longest-ever shows.

Those who were present that evening never forgot the tension of waiting for the star. Most of the acts who had volunteered to fill in had a tough job. And none more so than the performers who had to appear late, coping with the rising restlessness of the house.

'In a situation of this character,' *Variety* reported, 'when a vaudeville act knows it is walking into an absolute frost, also knowing that many of the profession are in front to witness the death, it really can be nothing short of courageous. Yet it was done by several, who sacrificed themselves for "stalling purposes".'

One artiste in particular did sterling work. He was Frank Tinney, who proved the riot of the evening at fifteen minutes past midnight. He had rushed down from the Winter Garden in his black-face make-up. His act helped considerably to keep the packed audience in the good humour that was necessary to stand the long wait. The great problem was to keep the customers happy, and to let them know that the great Harry Lauder would not be much longer in arriving.

Carter De Haven was the official master of ceremonies during the evening, and went on himself to sing a 'coon song'. The danger was that it was a number that had already been sung twice during the evening. Luckily, the audience bore with him.

'Don't worry,' they were told at 12.45, 'Mr Harry Lauder is almost with us. He has arrived at the Battery.'

Then Harry Cooper went forward to announce that 'Mister Lauder is now racing uptown in a machine.'

He added: 'While we are waiting for the star of our show, the gentlemen of the orchestra will play a few of the Scotchman's best-loved airs.'

The suspense, as they say, was 'killing'. Everybody realised that Harry Lauder would have to show up within a very few moments, or the whole house would empty. Anxious as they were to see and hear him, they could hardly go on waiting all night.

During the overture, Harry Cooper and Carter De Haven rushed back on stage, wildly waving their hands and yelling: 'He's here! Harry Lauder's here.'

Fortunately, he was. Right behind them, one second later, at precisely 12.56 am, came William Morris, hugging his breathless star from Scotland.

Harry Lauder paused dramatically, and made a speech. He thanked the audience for having waited. It was thanks genuinely expressed, for what a wonderful tribute their long wait had been to the charm and magic he seemed to cast over Americans as a whole.

Then a few books with his music were handed down to the musicians. It was the only property Lauder had been allowed to remove from the boat in his frantic dash to keep his appointment at the Manhattan Opera House.

'Aye, aye, I'm tellin' you, it's been a verra frantic rush,' Harry told his admirers. 'But now, if you will bear with me, I will go through the programme of songs I did at the ship's concert out in the Atlantic last Saturday night.'

86

The four songs he sang were all new to New York. *Every Laddie Loves A Lassie* was the first. Then came *Roamin' In The Gloamin'*, a success at the pantomime in the Glasgow Theatre Royal the previous winter, and destined to be one of his all-time hits. A Scottish marching song was the third. The orchestra, despite the emergency, played well, and the first two songs were received with a great ovation. Their catchy melodies, in Lauder's quaint old-fashioned style, proved popular. Harry registered as strongly as ever, and nobody present seemed to care that it was actually one o'clock in the morning! The house was enjoying itself to the full.

Among the volunteers on the bill earlier that historic night was Bob Fitzsimmons, the boxer, who came on very late and received a tremendous ovation. Another support artiste was a young singer already making a name for himself with his own compositions, name of – Irving Berlin.

Harry Lauder often talked of that late-late-late show he did at the Manhattan Opera House, but he didn't experience, at first-hand, the tremendous strain his absence and delay created on all concerned. As one observer put it, when ten o'clock came and no Harry Lauder, it seemed as if the audience 'might explode at any moment'.

Even in a modern age, with great fan followings for many singers in many lands, one doubts if any present-day audience would sit patiently for so long just to see their favourite star. Certainly not until one o'clock in the wee sma' hours of the morning!

That they did for a great Scot called Harry Lauder speaks volumes in itself.

A Tragic Telegram

IN THE LATE autumn of 1916 Harry Lauder was booked into a revue called *Three Cheers*, which duly opened at the Shaftesbury Theatre in the West End of London. It was midway through the period of the 1914–18 hostilities known in Europe as the Great War, and thousands of Servicemen on leave in London crowded in for an hour or two to find some diversion from the more serious business afoot.

The German Zeppelins were starting to raid London and England, and entertainment kept people's minds off the sad things. The merry little kilted Scots comedian-singer was just the chap to fill the bill at the Shaftesbury, packing into his act the kind of happy songs a soldier loved, as well as sufficient patriotic fervour to satisfy everyone. In one memorable scene Harry Lauder sang the number *The Laddies Who Fought And Won*, and it became a highspot of the revue.

As the song ended, a company of Scots Guards, in full-dress uniform, marched bravely on to the stage, and were given a thunderous ovation. Patriotism for king and country was in the air.

Each evening, as he sang that song, Harry Lauder found his own thoughts straying far away from the Shaftesbury Theatre, and across the sea to France, where his own son was in the fighting line. Captain John Lauder was with his regiment, the 8th Argyll and Sutherland Highlanders, at the battlefront in France.

This was the same John, Harry and Nance Lauder's only laddie, who had accompanied his father on that memorable first trip to America nine years previously. Now he was facing the enemy, and how Harry wished he could be beside him now! He would be twenty-three on his next birthday.

His mother and father had seen him off from the Central Station in Glasgow on the 16th September. John's bonnie Scots sweetheart, the girl he was to marry the following January when he came home on leave, had been there as well. It had been a sad farewell, for John had returned to the quiet of his home in Dunoon to recuperate from war nerves; now the line of duty called.

The late-autumn and winter months wore on, and Christmas 1916 dawned to find millions all over the world thinking dearly of their loved ones in uniform at the front.

New Year's Eve – or Hogmanay, as the Scots prefer to call it – came with a great wave of sentiment, and the crowds toasting-in the fresh New Year in the homes of relatives and friends from the Clyde to the Thames looked forward with hope to better times ahead.

Harry Lauder was staying that season at the Bonnington Hotel in London. He saw the New Year in by himself, having spent the earlier part of Hogmanay night with his manager and brother-in-law, Tom Vallance, at his home in Clapham. He wanted to get to bed early, ready for the show next afternoon.

The morning of the 1st January 1917 dawned, and Harry was joined in the hotel lounge for morning coffee by his good friends, Denis Clarke and his wife, from Birkenhead. Denis was the owner of the popular Argyle Theatre and the man who had given Lauder his early start in England; he was a personal friend of the family.

They ordered coffee in the lounge of the Bonnington, and talked about the show at the Shaftesbury. Suddenly, one of the hotel page-boys appeared beside their table.

'Mr Lauder, sir?' he said. The boy handed him a telegram, and Harry's face went ashen-grey as he frantically tore open the envelope, fearing – in fact, already knowing – that the worst had happened.

The Scot had, somehow, had a premonition. 'It's our John,' he gasped out, reading the telegram.

The piece of paper fluttered gently to the hotel floor. Couched in impersonal, official language, it stated: CAPTAIN JOHN LAUDER KILLED IN ACTION DECEMBER 28TH OFFICIAL WAR OFFICE

At that moment in time, on a New Year's Day when hope and happiness should have been in the air for all, the world collapsed around Harry Lauder, the gay singing minstrel whose job was to make others happy. His friends rallied to his side as he wept bitterly.

Harry's first thought was to be beside his wife, who had stayed behind for Hogmanay at their home in Dunoon, in Scotland. Reading the telegram again, he saw that it had been despatched from the post office at Dunoon, on the Clyde. Then Nance must have sent it. She must already have the news. Poor Nance, all alone with her heartbreak! Harry knew he simply had to get up there and stay beside her at this hour.

Out of respect to the gallant wee Scot, the management closed down the revue *Three Cheers* until further notice. They realised that it would be impossible for any star to go out and laugh and sing in the circumstances. Lauder must be given time to recover from the sad and tragic blow.

That night, with his manager Tom Vallance, he went up to Glasgow on the midnight express. Next morning he arrived at the Lauder home near Dunoon. Fortunately, Nance was taking the terrible blow courageously and with great calm. Together, she and Harry sat and prayed. They could say so little. Their thoughts were far away – on that battlefield in Europe, where their only son lay dead. The couple knelt down and prayed again.

'We're not alone in our tragedy,' Nance reminded her husband. 'We forget, Harry, that we are just one set of parents among thousands for whom the blow has struck. Let's remember that. Think of the thousands, no millions, of fathers and mothers who have received similar telegrams.'

Next day Harry thought of the show he had left in the heart of London. He knew he really had to face life and go back. But how could he do it? How, possibly, could he ever go out again in front of hundreds of people, and laugh and sing and pretend to be happy?

He talked it over – as he did everything – with Nance.

'Of course, Harry, you must go back,' she told him. 'Think what this show means to so many. If it has to fold, it will put hundreds out of work they badly need.

'You've a duty to your fellow-professionals, and you know that. And a duty to the public as well. Entertainment is priority work in any war, Harry.'

Lauder decided to return to London, and his manager Tom booked his seat on the Glasgow–London express. Three nights later he was being whisked through the January night, back to London town. But it was still a great ordeal to face. He dreaded the thought of walking on to that stage again in the midst of his great grief.

When he reached the theatre, a letter was handed to him by special messenger. It had come from a fellow-officer who was with his son when he was killed. The Captain, he told him, had died with great gallantry, calling out the words: 'Carry on!'

There were hundreds of other letters and messages of sympathy, many scrawled in shaky handwriting by old and lonely folk among his fans. There were letters from the high and important ones in the land. But that simple message from France and the battlefront left Harry Lauder, heartbroken parent, in no further doubt as to what he must do. He must 'Carry on'. The show must go on.

It was a theatre moment never to forget as Lauder, the little Scotsman, sad at heart but forcing a smile, stood in the wings of the Shaftesbury Theatre awaiting his cue. From the moment he entered there was an immediate bond of sympathy between audience and performer, rare in theatre. Harry stood there in the spotlight as the audience cheered and cheered. The house was packed. He sang *I Love My Jean*, and then almost had to go off, so choked was he inside.

The big scene for Lauder was the one where the Scots Guards marched on to the stage and he sang about *The Laddies Who Fought And Won*. It had a deep and personal significance for him that night.

Lord Alness, from Edinburgh, who was in the theatre audience that historic evening, later recalled the moment. 'I can remember him still,' he said of Lauder. 'His face had a fixed look as he sang. I really don't think he saw his audience. But the show, in the traditional phrase, went on.'

Harry just managed to get through the number about 'A' The Lassies Lovin' A' The Laddies, The Laddies Who Fought And Won'. But he broke down slightly when he came to sing the lines

When we all gather round the old fireside,
And the fond mother kisses her son . . .

He recovered quickly, however, and then led the audience in the singing of *God Save The King*. And then, as the curtain finally came down, he fainted.

Lauder's wife travelled south to join him in London after that, and together they did valuable work for hospitals all over the south of England. Harry and Nance were to learn that there is nothing in life like taking an interest in the sorrows of others for taking your mind off your own.

As the weeks went past, Harry worked out a plan. It was obvious he was trying to keep the secret to himself. At last he came out with it, as usual, to Nance. He was thinking seriously of joining up in the army himself. He might be all of forty-seven years old, but older men had done it. So he volunteered.

'Sorry, Mr Lauder, but you're too old,' they told him.

'Right, then,' replied Lauder, 'let me sing to the boys. I'm tellin' you, let me go right to the fighting line and get in among them. I'm an entertainer . . . I can make their load a wee bit lighter wi' a sang or two, and a joke or two.

'It's the least I can do for memory o' John.'

There was lots of official talk and argument. Then, at the end of May 1917, the important letter arrived from the War Office, giving Harry the go-ahead. He was to travel across to France and move around among the Scottish troops – the Argylls, the Black Watch, the Camerons, the Gordons and the Highland Light Infantry.

So Harry and his party of entertainers sailed off. They left from Folkestone on a June day. Harry took with him a portable piano, and thousands of packets of cigarettes for the Scots abroad. Their first show was given at the Casino in Boulogne, France, which was serving as a base hospital. The troops loved the energetic little Scots star, of whom they had heard so much.

Wherever Lauder moved in France, he set up his portable piano and sang the well-loved songs the soldiers knew so well. Sometimes the show would take place in a fine old French château, still safe from enemy attack; sometimes it would go on in the yard of a sleepy French farm. At other times audiences of kilted 'Jocks' sat in pillaged barns or even in dug-outs.

The Lauder songs had a special appeal to troops far from their own homes and friends and firesides. For he sang to them of love and bonnie lassies and that dear wee hoose 'mang the heather. These were the basics of life. Those Service audiences wanted to be reminded of home and loved ones. Harry was the lad to do it.

One of his early shows took place in a never-to-be-forgotten setting. It was in the Château of Tramecourt, a dignified old French mansion which an equally dignified French lady and her daughter had refused to quit despite the onrush of war.

It must have been a truly memorable scene as Scottish officers in the kilt and tartan greeted the great music-hall star in that tasteful drawing-room, lit only by candles, and as Harry Lauder, in his unmistakable Scottish burr, raised his glass and toasted 'our brave French hostess and her charming daughter'.

Lauder went on to Albert and Arras, and down to Péronne. He gave half a dozen shows a day, his audiences varying from tiny units of a hundred to vast gatherings some three thousand strong. For one concert at Arras it was estimated there were over five thousand men waiting to hear and see him one summer's evening in June.

Airplanes were sent up to keep off the Germans while Harry Lauder got on with his job of singing. At one stage on the tour the minstrel was allowed to fire a British gun himself.

Wherever he travelled at the front, he met friends. Some had even been at school with him in Scotland. Others had been miners in the pits he knew so well in Lanarkshire. The really moving moment of the tour came when Harry reached at last the little war cemetery at Ovilliers, on the Albert–Péronne road. There he was led to the grave of his son, Captain John Lauder, of the Argyll and Sutherland Highlanders, *Killed in Action, December 28, 1916.*

Harry Lauder took off his Balmoral bonnet, knelt on the green grass, and said a silent prayer. He remained on that precious piece of ground for the next twenty minutes, memories flooding back to him.

Then, wiping a tear from his eye, he walked briskly back to his party, ready to 'carry on' with the show. As always through life the show must go on, and the great little Scottish trouper was ready for action again.

As a worker for war charities, Harry Lauder had few equals. He was fired by a great desire to work and slave and spare no effort so that the enemy would finally be destroyed. The death of his son was constantly in his mind.

He called his fund 'The Harry Lauder Million-Pound Fund for Maimed Men, Scottish Soldiers and Sailors'. It was launched soon after he returned from his visit to the front line, and the organisers went into action on the 17th September 1917.

Lauder was anxious that it wouldn't clash with any other similar schemes, and he had a private session with the Minister of Pensions in London before he went ahead.

A music-hall star in the year 1917 had the ear of the British public to a very great degree. But Harry Lauder, vaudeville minstrel star, had another great advantage. He had been touring the great North American continent for ten years, and knew literally thousands of important and influential people in the USA.

'If Harry Lauder can't raise money for war charities, then I don't know who can,' he said, with genuine pride.

So he sailed again for America, launched into yet another concert tour, and, at the close of each performance, went forward to the footlights and told his audience what he wanted and the object of his Harry Lauder Fund.

The exiled Scots in his audiences were most generous. So were the Americans. Very often people in the circle would toss money down to Harry on the stage below. Others would hand in their dollars at the stage-door, with a request that they go to the Harry Lauder Million-Pound Fund.

Nance stood out in the theatre foyer after each show and sold little envelopes with tartan borders, containing stamps. The proceeds went to help the Fund.

The generosity of America was considerable, and the goodwill of his hundreds of audiences – strangers as well as friends – touched Harry deeply. People who obviously could ill afford to add a contribution sent in their dollars. At Hot Springs, in Arkansas, the stage-hands at the theatre sacrificed the pay they earned during Lauder's engagement to hand it over to his Fund.

Harry Lauder was a persuasive speaker. His natural, unaffected Scottish way of talking drove his points right home. There was nobody in those audiences who could possibly doubt his great sincerity.

One particularly memorable meeting was held in the Hippodrome in New York. Many of the city's notables were on the platform. Harry talked at length, and described in some detail his visits to France. He was careful to stress the feminine angle, there being hundreds of American women in that audience.

'Wonderful, wonderful, Mr Lauder'. 'You were great, Harry'. 'You can talk even better than you sing'. Comments such as these were common when the gathering had ended.

Harry rarely let up in his tremendous zeal to put over the war story from Britain. He addressed meetings by the dozen and attended Rotary Clubs by the score. All this was in addition to his normal variety concerts in the evenings.

At many gatherings Harry joined forces with the National Security League of America. He gave and secured co-operation wherever he went.

Travelling up to Montreal, he spoke at a Rotary Club luncheon in the city and remarked on the possibility that people of French

Lauder in the late 1920s.

Number 3 Bridge Street, Portobello, where
Harry Lauder was born in August 1870.

Lauder Ha'.

Four Lauder character studies.

Photos: The Scotsman

The Scotsman

At St Andrews with Mr John
MacDonald, the son of the agent
who gave Harry his first chance
on the concert platform.

With his wife and son, John,
Lauder stands beside his Nagant–
Hobson car. At the wheel is Tom
Vallance, his brother-in-law and
manager. *The Scotsman*

Harry Lauder with a group of Scottish music-hall comedians. Among them (*back row*) Charlie Kemble, Bert Denver, Dave Willis, Jack Anthony, Jack Radcliffe. (*Front row*) Will Fyffe, Lauder, Harry Gordon.

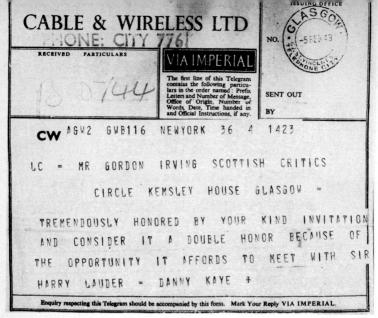

CABLE & WIRELESS LTD
PHONE: CITY 7761
RECEIVED PARTICULARS
VIA IMPERIAL

The first line of this Telegram contains the following particulars in the order named : Prefix Letter and Number of Message, Office of Origin, Number of Words, Date, Time handed in and Official Instructions, if any.

ISSUING OFFICE GLASGOW
NO.
SENT OUT
BY

13 0744

CW AGW2 GWB116 NEWYORK 36 4 1423

LC = MR GORDON IRVING SCOTTISH CRITICS

CIRCLE KEMSLEY HOUSE GLASGOW =

TREMENDOUSLY HONORED BY YOUR KIND INVITATION

AND CONSIDER IT A DOUBLE HONOR BECAUSE OF

THE OPPORTUNITY IT AFFORDS TO MEET WITH SIR

HARRY LAUDER = DANNY KAYE +

Enquiry respecting this Telegram should be accompanied by this form. Mark Your Reply VIA IMPERIAL.

Telegram from Danny Kaye to the author which resulted in the historic meeting and friendship between Lauder and Kaye.

The family circle at Lauder Ha'. Greta, Lauder's niece, Harry, and Danny Kaye, with Mr Alf Ellsworth, a family friend.

The proud moment at Buckingham Palace in April 1919 when Harry and Nance leave as Sir Harry and Lady Lauder. *The Scotsman*

Sir Harry off to a garden party at Buckingham Palace. *The Scotsman*

Lauder is given the Freedom of Edinburgh in the Usher Hall, 1927. Beside him is an empty chair out of respect to Lady Lauder who had just died. *The Scotsman*

Lauder's collection of twirly sticks, ready for auction at Lauder Ha'.

Harry's faithful niece and companion Miss Greta Lauder at her desk in Lauder Ha'.

The Lauder family's tomb-stone records the history from his parents' deaths to Harry's own in 1950.

Ford

blood in Eastern Canada were perhaps not helping their home country as they might in the bitter struggle against the enemy.

The Press took up the points in his address, and hundreds of French-Canadians looked on the Lauder speech as an attack on them. Their anger became so great that trouble, in fact, was anticipated. Harry was even urged to keep to his hotel suite and to cancel his week's show at His Majesty's Theatre in the city.

'No, no!' he declared, to friends who suggested this would be the wiser course. 'I've told the truth, I know what I'm talking about, and I'm not afraid of any man, French-Canadian or not.

'My speech has been made, and my show will go on. I'm not going back on my word.'

To show he meant what he said, Lauder donned his kilt and Balmoral bonnet, and went walking down St Catherine Street. Many comments of abuse and derogation were tossed at him, but he ignored them all and was not seized on or attacked, as many thought he would be.

Just in case of any emergency, however, a security guard was placed outside his hotel, and troops were kept standing by the theatre where the Harry Lauder show was playing. A packed audience gave him a warm reception, and there was no further outburst during the week.

Harry Lauder had great personal sympathy for soldiers who had lost a leg or an arm, or their sight, in the bloody struggle in Europe. He had personally met and talked with scores of these lads, and wondered how they could be helped on their return to civvy street, their whole lives thus shattered. He had been greatly impressed by their courage as he sang to them in army camps and hospitals.

Young men like these, he kept saying, must not be tossed back into life and left to their own devices. They must never be forgotten by the nation. It would be tragic indeed if they had to stand at street corners selling books of matches or begging for money.

Then there were the shell-shocked and the paralysed and those who were completely blind, all because they had gone out to help their country in time of war.

The Press took up the cause, and Lauder's campaign gained the necessary publicity. It had the Earl of Rosebery as its honorary president, and Lord Balfour of Burleigh as its treasurer. There was support for it from every side.

'The Harry Lauder Million-Pound Fund' proved a worthwhile cause in the last year of the European conflagration. Many of the lads who fought and won (but came home with badly wounded and disfigured bodies) had cause to be grateful for its help.

Congratulations, Sir Harry

HARRY LAUDER WAS always intensely proud of his many meetings
with the Presidents of the United States of America. It gave him,
an ordinary Scotsman from the coalfields of his own land, a great
thrill to know that they had heard of and appreciated his variety
act, and were more than willing to meet him away from the
theatre – as a sort of ambassador for the land of Auld Lang Syne
and, indeed, for Great Britain as a whole.

President Theodore Roosevelt was a special favourite with the
variety star. Harry was happy to meet 'Teddy', as he knew him,
on several occasions during his term of office from 1901 to 1909.

He remembered him as an American who obviously knew his
mind, and who looked straight at you to reveal an earnest and
sincere character. Lauder always recalled that 'Teddy' had broad
and strong-looking shoulders.

What impressed him most, however, was that this particular
American President had a fine sense of humour and could laugh
heartily at jokes, especially those against himself and the Americans.

Harry Lauder didn't get himself involved to any depth in
American politics, but he could never fully understand why so
many Americans either went completely overboard in their support of 'Teddy' Roosevelt or the whole hog in their condem-
nation of him.

President Theodore Roosevelt left a lasting impression on the
mind of the visiting Scottish entertainer, who summed him up as

a man of determination and iron, keen and able to overcome all difficulties.

They met socially on several occasions, and 'Teddy' Roosevelt was always intrigued to know more about the colourful and romantic world of showbusiness in which Lauder moved, and about his home and friends in Scotland.

Sometimes it was on the golf course that Lauder met these first citizens of America. He was a keen golfer, and claimed that 'hitting the wee gutty ba' ' was one of his favourite relaxations. Harry had never lost interest in the game to which he had been first introduced as a wee laddie and caddie, when he carried the clubs of the wealthy gentlemen from Edinburgh on the links at Musselburgh.

He once played a game of golf with President William H Taft at Augusta, in Georgia, and actually beat the President by two holes. Bill Taft was a tall and amply-built man, contrasting oddly in size with the wee and wiry Harry. Lauder admired Taft as a man, and always remembered the genial and pleasant way he smiled at life.

Harry and Nance were regularly invited to the White House in Washington to meet the then-President of the United States.

The pleasant American custom of taking breakfast with your host intrigued Harry and his wife immensely. It meant you had to be up bright and early, and he admired this early-rising trait in all the top Americans he met, in business, politics or the theatre. He had always been used to early-rising himself, and was delighted to find it one of the hallmarks of the success of the good folk of the USA.

President Warren G Harding, with whom he played golf at the Congressional Golf Course in Washington, welcomed Harry and Nance to the White House, and laughed and cracked jokes about Scotland and America over a magnificent breakfast-plateful of fried ham and eggs, Harry's favourite morning dish.

President Harding talked to Harry about his native state of Ohio, and was tickled pink when Harry said he would write 'a wee song' about the state. Ohio had just the right kind of sound for a line in a Scottish song, Harry told him, and he was as good as his word, bringing the colourful-sounding name into one of his best-known numbers.

Calvin Coolidge and Woodrow Wilson were other friends of the Lauders through meetings at the White House. President Wilson was anxious to meet Harry for one particular reason. He wanted to thank him for all the grand work he was doing in helping to entertain the troops during the war.

The first Harry Lauder-Woodrow Wilson meeting took place in Washington when the Scots singer visited there during his American tour of 1917. The President and his wife sat in the audience at one of Harry's most successful shows, and joined enthusiastically in the applause for the kilted Scot. They sent round a message with an official inviting him to the White House for tea before his tour ended, and Harry was able to accept during that week.

Lauder had returned from his visit to the front line in France, and had gone to America mainly as an entertainer but partly to tell the people of the United States how gallantly Britain was fighting the war. He had sailed aboard the *Mauretania*, defying the day and night menace of prowling U-boats.

The entire organisation of the American Young Men's Christian Association was put at his disposal to allow him to talk to the youth of America. Harry addressed one vast gathering on a Sunday night in the New York Hippodrome, and another, with many thousands present, in the vast Civic Auditorium in San Francisco, California.

He was a persuasive speaker and lightened his talks with little bits of humour and stories from the fighting line.

Audiences, just as in the theatre, were with him all the way.

One, in the open air in Wall Street, New York, was estimated at over two hundred thousand strong. The enthusiasm of the Americans for the war effort in Europe was great.

Always, Harry had the image of his son John before him. He remembered particularly how, as a mere schoolboy, John had accompanied him on his very first visit to this great country, and he thought of him lying dead on the battlefield and buried in that faraway grave at Ovilliers.

Wherever he toured in the America of late 1917, Lauder devoted his time and energies to talking about Britain and the war in Europe. He visited thousands of young Americans training for the combat, and sang his songs to them. He travelled across the continent from coast to coast, sparing no effort in his propaganda. He was a popular figure with the American Serviceman.

Only in communities where he found a sizable German element did he encounter opposition and, on occasion, violent threats. As a rule, he found nothing but enthusiasm and support for Britain right across America and up in Eastern Canada, which he also visited.

Lauder was always very proud of a little poem which an American lady, Amelia J Burr, wrote about him in the columns of a weekly magazine, the *New York Outlook*, in 1917.

It was headed: THE FIERY CROSS. It was dedicated to Harry Lauder, and the first verse read:

He stood behind the footlights, and he set the crowd a-laughing
With the same old crooning chuckle that we loved in other years,
And only those who knew could guess the grief behind the daffing,
But, for those who did, the laughter had a secret salt of tears.
Then at the last he came out in his grass-green coat and bonnet,
With his gaudy tartans coloured like a garden in the sun,
The same quaint little figure – but a different face was on it
When he sang about the laddies that so well had fought and won.

Harry carried a clipping of that poem in his sporran for many years. It summed up for him the gratitude of millions of Americans whom he had met and talked with on his tour. It left him in no doubt as to the great respect in which they held him, as a man as well as a variety star.

Back home again from his travels, both in America and at the front, Mr Harry Lauder, tired and weary after so much good work for the war effort, was as relieved as anyone in Europe when the Armistice was signed in November 1918. The war years had dealt him a devastating personal blow in the death of his only son, but, like so many others in Britain, he had rallied with the gallantry that dominated his whole life, and he was still keeping right on to the end of the road.

Little did he realise then, with the first European war over, that he was to live through yet a second world war two decades later. And entertain in that one too.

The soldiers came marching home again from France, many of them singing the lilting Lauder tunes, and soon a' the lassies were a-lovin' a' the laddies, the laddies who had fought and won. Harry Lauder had certainly done his bit in the war effort.

With peace declared, he set off immediately for America – and another tour. He sailed with Mrs Lauder on the *Mauretania* two days after the gunfire in Europe ceased. It was the same liner that had carried him across to America through the U-boat menace in 1917.

The following March, in 1919, he went on to Australia, and was in the city of Sydney, having lunch in the Hotel Australia, when once again a cablegram reached him.

Telegrams and cables always seemed to come to Harry at dramatic points in his life and career. This one was handed to his manager, Tom Vallance, who read it quietly, then held out his hand.

He smiled, and said: 'Congratulations, *Sir* Harry! Then, turning to his sister Nancy, he said: 'Nance, my dear, you are now Lady Lauder.'

It was a moment for Lauder and his wife to remember for the rest of their lives. Harry kissed Nance, and everybody was highly excited. The other diners in the room joined in the congratulations. Toasts were drunk to the new knight and his lady.

This was, indeed, theatrical history in the making. For the first time an artiste of the music-hall, as distinct from the legitimate theatre, was being honoured by his king and country.

King George the Fifth had been pleased to confer on Mr Lauder a Knighthood of the British Empire. Harry had worked hard to keep the boys at the front happy, he had done sterling work in propaganda in America, and now he was being honoured with high new rank for services rendered. It was well deserved.

The great little minstrel found it hard to keep back a tear. His joy (and that of his beloved Nance) would surely have been complete if only his son John had been spared to share the honour with him.

Knighthood for a showbusiness star was headline news that Easter in Australia. Audiences went out of their way to cheer the wee Scot not only for his performance in the theatre, but also for the high honour he had gained. Sir Harry – he could hardly get used to the new title – found it all extremely moving.

Those struggling days of boyhood and poverty in the wee house in Portobello, near Edinburgh, seemed so far away, and yet so near. If only his mother could see him now!

The news of the award went right round the world, as indeed, it always did when Harry Lauder was in the limelight. Very soon the messages of congratulation and good wishes were pouring back in over the wires. They came from all parts of the globe, and Sir Harry and Tom Vallance spent two full weeks acknowledging them. Even that was not sufficient time to cope with them all.

Memories of his past came flooding back to Lauder during that fortnight in Sydney. He thought again of the wee 'but an' ben' where he had been brought up in Portobello, by the Firth of Forth. He thought of his mother and father, struggling so hard to bring up the large family of boys and girls. He thought of his days in the flax-mill at Arbroath, of his days and nights down the coal mines near Hamilton, of the time in London when he had almost despaired of making the grade as a comedian.

He thought back to the day he had first stepped ashore in New York, John by his side, and nervously faced his first American audience. He remembered the so-recent New Year's Day in London when the fateful telegram came informing him that John had been killed at the front. All these and many more memories came rushing back. Now the present and the future faced him, and he was no longer plain 'Mister Lauder' but a true knight of the realm, Sir Harry Lauder.

He was quite overwhelmed when he went to Buckingham Palace in London with his dear Nance in April of that year – and they emerged to meet the waiting photographers as Sir Harry and Lady Lauder.

Eight years later, in 1927, there was to come an equally proud moment in Harry's career and life.

He was called to the capital city of Edinburgh, not so very far from his humble birthplace at Portobello, to receive the Freedom of the City at a memorable gathering in the city's Usher Hall.

It was another great occasion for Lauder. Boys and girls from Edinburgh schools were on the platform.

But there was one very touching gesture about that ceremony. A chair close to the city's Lord Provost was kept empty. It was in memory of Lady Lauder, Harry's beloved Nance, who had died suddenly in Glasgow not long before that Freedom day. How sad that she did not live to share it!

It had previously been agreed that no songs were to be included in the Freedom ceremony. Then, as it transpired, Sir Harry ended his touching speech with a reference to his famous song *Keep Right On To The End Of The Road*.

This was a cue that no audience, let alone a Scottish one, could ignore. Anyhow, what good was Harry Lauder without a song! All the very important folk in that great Usher Hall, and all the ordinary citizens of Scotland's capital, joined in as Lauder, in grand voice, led them in the singing of his immortal song.

There was an amusing moment when Lauder stopped the organist and then started afresh in his own key, leaving the organist to follow him.

The Freedom Casket from Edinburgh, with its treasured scroll, was given an honoured place among the Lauder souvenirs and relics. It was something Sir Harry prized very highly. The great capital city of Scotland had at last honoured the laddie born in a poor home in the neighbouring town of Portobello.

Harry Lauder made twenty-two visits to America and the publicity they received somewhat obscured the pleasures of his trips to Australia and New Zealand. These, again, were for the specific purpose of singing to and appearing before the exiled Scots and, once again, they resulted in the little Scotsman becoming the darling of the great Australian and New Zealand public as a whole.

It was from America, in 1911, that the name and fame of Lauder spread across the Pacific to showbusiness agents and representatives in Australia. They kept asking him to accept a booking. Harry felt a duty to the Scots both there and in New Zealand.

Fittingly, then, it was from the west coast of America that he started out for this new continent, sailing from San Francisco on a brisk February morning in 1914. An interesting and most lucrative theatrical season in Australia and New Zealand lay ahead; it was another challenge to the Scot.

But there were really relaxing days for Harry. After the whipped-up frenzy and enthusiasm of the North Americans, it was a pleasant change to embark leisurely on board ship, and lap up all the romance of the world as you made your way, slowly and surely, across another ocean to a land that Scots had often talked about, at home and in the USA.

Lauder was always the ever-grateful traveller. He never ceased to marvel that here he was, once a poor and humble lad with scarcely a penny or cent to his name, sailing in luxury to new, romantic and glamorous places and new faces. He used to take a wee stroll on deck before turning in, and would put up a grateful prayer of thanks to God for giving him such wonderful opportunities to see the world – and be paid for it at the same time!

His first sight of the new continent was of Sydney Harbour in all its magnificence. The publicity machine had been working overtime, and nobody was left in any doubt that the great entertainer from Scotland, Harry Lauder, already the toast of America, was arriving that morning. Ships blew their sirens to welcome him in, and bands played gaily in the streets as Lauder made his well-timed entrance. Hundreds of Scottish exiles living in Sydney and other parts of New South Wales were there to cheer him that March morning.

It was truly a red-letter day in the life of New South Wales, as the Press writers of the time duly chronicled it in their Sydney newspapers. The Press of Australia waxed almost as enthusiastic over the visiting Scotsman as their colleagues in the USA had done when he first arrived in New York.

Harry duly opened on Easter Saturday at the Theatre Royal

in Sydney, and the Australians' welcome was as warm and ardent as ever any in America had been. He was contracted to play a four-weeks' season in Sydney, and he could easily have stayed on for another month. The box-office registered capacity business all the time. Lauder was the big talking-point in shops, offices and warehouses – and out on the sheep stations in the hinterland.

From Sydney Harry travelled on to Melbourne, and there it was the same wonderful story – cheers all the way. Everyone went wild about little Harry, and yet another theatre notched up standing-room-only business for a month. He couldn't help being a success. Then it was on to Adelaide and Brisbane and other cities of Australia. Enthusiastic welcomes awaited him everywhere.

Lauder often said this was the happiest period of his life. He was in his forty-fourth year, at the height of his strength and talents, and everything was going swimmingly. Nance was enjoying the tour with him, they were meeting kind and hospitable people, and life was going like a song.

To cap it all, the Lauders' son John was to sail out to join his parents in Australia when his term ended for the summer vacation at Cambridge University, where he was studying for his Bachelor of Arts degree and a career as a London barrister.

In the meantime, Harry and Nance crossed over to New Zealand, and spent six happy weeks there, playing before hundreds of Scottish exiles in the principal towns. Then they sailed back to Australia to welcome their son, who was by now arriving after the long sea voyage from Britain.

It was a difficult and critical time for Great Britain; dark war clouds had been gathering over Europe, menacing and ominous.

John Lauder stepped on to Australian territory on the 31st July, and had four happy days with his parents. They tried not to talk about the increasingly darkening war situation, which seemed so far distant in Europe, but it wasn't easy.

Then on the 4th August 1914 – Harry Lauder's own forty-fourth birthday, as it happened – the news broke. The newsboys shouted it in the streets. The mother country, Great Britain, was at war with Germany. The Lauder family heard the grim news as they sat in their hotel over lunch.

It was a time of much anxiety and worry for the Lauders, so happy to be together at last in this friendly land. On the 5th August a cable arrived for John. It asked him to rejoin his regiment, the Argyll and Sutherland Highlanders, back at their depot in Britain. A passage home was arranged, and within another few days Harry and Nance's son was en route to England again, his long-anticipated visit to Australia so cruelly cut short.

He had seen his mother and father off by ship to Wellington in New Zealand, where they were continuing the tour. Then, with a friend, he caught a train to Adelaide, and sailed from there to England.

Harry Lauder himself was also on the move again in that fateful August of 1914. After a few weeks in New Zealand, he sailed back across the Pacific to San Francisco, and resumed an autumn and winter tour of the United States. But his heart was really thousands of miles away with his son in Britain, now stationed at Bedford, in England, with the 51st Highland Division.

In his career, Harry was to acquire a fairly close working knowledge of Australia and its kindly people, making four tours of the country in all. He developed a great liking for its pleasant climate and its fine cities. He played in most of the important centres of Victoria, Queensland, New South Wales and Western Australia and, in leisure moments, visited sheep farms and goldmining communities.

Just as he had become friendly with the Presidents of the United States of America, so doors were opened to Lauder in this new country, and he came to know personally the Prime Ministers of

Australia, often playing golf with them during his tours.

The leisurely trip across the Pacific from Australia to America and its sunny western coast was the favourite sea voyage for Harry Lauder. He loved calling in at places like Samoa or Honolulu, and he came to regret, he said, that he had never been a sailor and seen the rest of the world.

Songs about the sea are fairly common in the Lauder songbooks, and many of these were composed by him in his cabin, or on deck, while crossing the Pacific, either going to or returning from another tour of Australia and New Zealand.

These were countries that left a lasting impression on Lauder the globe-trotting Scot. His name is still an honoured one among the great-grandchildren of the men and women who were his audiences at the time.

As his fame increased and spread to different corners of the world, Harry Lauder, now proudly bearing the title of Sir Harry, found that, more and more, his life was not his own. He was now a public figure, and even people who had never seen him before were at harbours and railroad stations to greet him like an old friend. They arrived hours before he was due, and lined the streets and barriers, or took up stances in high buildings, to welcome the famous entertainer.

His knighthood, of course, had much to do with this. The news of it had been splashed in newspapers all over the world, and had given him a fresh fame. Then there were his gramophone records; these were selling fast in different countries, and had made his voice and his comedy act a familiar and popular one even before he had been seen in person in certain towns and cities.

In 1920 Lauder sailed out to South Africa to make his bow there. As he walked down the gangway from the ship, the crowds cheered. There were about three thousand people to welcome him in Cape Town, and he had to face all the fuss and publicity, and answer questions by the dozen from the city's newspapermen.

Harry often found himself puzzled by the strength of welcomes like these. He couldn't forget that he was only a simple Scotsman and a music-hall comedian, somebody who had done little – so he modestly thought – to improve the human lot.

The scenes in Cape Town were enthusiastic, almost frenzied. Lauder was mobbed in his hotel and on the streets. The management of the theatre where he played was delighted, and had to put out the 'House Full' boards. Lauder, in fact, found it difficult to get off the stage each evening, and this despite the fact that he did an act lasting well over seventy-five minutes.

Talk about one-man shows! Stars like Maurice Chevalier, Danny Kaye and Max Bygraves, in later years, were only following in the wake of Lauder. He was the original pioneer of the one-man charm-'em solo school of entertainment.

Today, when headline variety artistes occupy the greater part of the second-half of any bill, audiences and critics rave, and people marvel at their talent. It is a pity they never saw Scotland's Harry Lauder at the height of his career!

As usual, South Africa was no different from the United States or Australia or London. It was the fashionable 'thing' for all the best and most important people to be seen at a Harry Lauder performance. The VIPs of Cape Town helped to swell the theatre, diamonds glittering, the best bib and tucker on show. They had heard or read that Lauder was very much favoured by British royalty, and were anxious to pay him their respects.

One evening the Governor-General, Lord Buxton, graced that Cape Town theatre audience with his presence, and asked to meet Harry Lauder at the end of the performance.

He was profuse in his praise. 'A most heart-warming entertainment, Sir Harry,' his Excellency told him, when the little Scot presented himself to his party in the Government box. 'We have already heard so much about you, and now we know it is all so true.

'Would you do the honour of lunching with me at Government House tomorrow?'

Lauder, of course, accepted. He was always thrilled to meet the top people in any country, although he was the first to admit that he did this purely on the basis of paying his own respects to the leaders of an overseas nation. He vehemently denied any charges – and they were, at times, levelled against him – of social snobbery.

In Cape Town he became the first British music-hall star to make the acquaintance of the Governor-General, and the visit of Sir Harry to Government House was quite a talking-point in that country.

Later, the tartan minstrel was practically given the freedom of the city, and was conducted on sight-seeing trips to all the places of historical interest. And of course, he had many meetings once again with exiled Scots.

The success-story of his tour was repeated all over South Africa. In Johannesburg he played his act to really amazing business. Hundreds were turned away each evening, and Harry stayed over for a full four-weeks' season, playing to record returns at the box-office.

One night, at his theatre in Durban, a Basuto doctor went round after the performance and asked if he could be introduced to Sir Harry. When he was shown in to the Lauder dressing-room, the wee Scot was most impressed and, need I add, highly flattered. For this coloured medical man who spoke excellent English surprised him with a most detailed knowledge of his career in the Scottish and English theatre.

'I have followed your progress all over the world, Sir Harry,' he told him. 'I've read all about your wonderful seasons in the United States of America. And, do you know something, sir, I pride myself that I was one of your earliest fans.

'You see, Sir Harry, I took my medical degree in Scotland. I was a student at Edinburgh University, and many a night's relaxation I got from my studies and books by buying a ticket for your performance at the Empire Theatre in Nicolson Street. They were happy days.'

Lauder's 1920 tour of South Africa helped make a lot of the fortune which he was able to enjoy in later life. In fact, it was during this trip that he collected the biggest week's salary he had earned to date, and put aside part of it to buy himself a spanking new Rolls-Royce motor-car on his return to London.

The early 1920s were again golden years for Lauder. With the war over, he seemed to want to work harder than ever, and to tour for even greater distances and longer seasons. There was relief for the Scot in work, and he threw himself into his career with even greater energy; it was one way of forgetting his own sadness and the death of his son John.

As he advised others so often, it was fatal for anybody to sit down and do nothing when tragedy knocked at the door. The best cure was to proceed immediately with the next job in hand, and to get so involved in activity that there was little time to feel sorry for yourself.

South Africa, America, Australia, New Zealand . . . the whole world was beckoning again to the minstrel star. He was determined to keep busy by making other people happy. His stamina was something that everyone admired.

Chaplin, and Other Friends

LAUDER WAS A man with millions of admirers but only a handful of really close friends. But those who had the honour of numbering themselves among the latter were true and genuine friends indeed.

One of them was Andrew Carnegie, the famous Scottish-born philanthropist, who had made good in America and was proud to welcome such a popular Great Scot to the land of his adoption. He was thirty-four years Harry's senior, and to him the sturdy singer and comedian from the Lanarkshire coalfields was no more than a laddie when he reached America. Andrew Carnegie felt it a duty to welcome him to the new country and to keep him on the right tracks.

There was quite a likeness in their two upbringings. Like Harry Lauder, Andrew Carnegie had been born in one of the smaller towns of Scotland – Dunfermline, in Fife. Like Harry, he also came from a humble background, his father's family having been handloom weavers for many generations in the east of Scotland. Carnegie, too, had seen hard work in a factory, in much the same way as Lauder had in the grim flax-mills of Arbroath. He had emigrated as a fourteen-year-old to Alleghany, in Pennsylvania, and had become a bobbin boy in a local cotton factory.

But fortune was rapid for Andrew Carnegie. At the age of twenty-four he became vice-president of the Pennsylvania Railroad, and started building up a small fortune. His best stroke of business was to invest in the booming United States iron industry, and eventually he invested his capital in a steel plant. By 1900, exactly seven years before Harry Lauder arrived in New York, Andrew Carnegie was producing one quarter of all the steel in the USA. The following year he sold his holdings to the Morgan Group for the amazing sum of 225 million dollars.

So, by the time the raw kilted entertainer laddie from Hamilton, in Lanarkshire, reached America, Carnegie was devoting his time and money to the advancement of education and of world peace.

Harry Lauder was first introduced to Carnegie when he called round to present his good wishes to the fellow-Scot in his dressing-room at Blaney's Theatre.

'I'm right happy to meet you, lad,' said the older man. 'You stand for all that's good and great about Scotsmen and Scotland, and you're putting it over in the way we all love. I know my America, lad, and you've hit them at the right time and in the right place – their hearts. They're tickled pink by your tartan naturalness, lad.'

Then Carnegie invited Lauder to visit him at his luxurious house in Fifth Avenue, New York. It was a revelation to the entertainer, who at that time had seen little of the world's luxury. He took away with him a memory of the most lavish and expensive home he had ever been inside in his life.

Carnegie was able to help Harry Lauder on his American treks. The people of the USA have the wonderful knack of introducing visitors to other persons who may be able to help them, and Andrew Carnegie, naturally, had more contacts and influence than most.

After long cracks into the wee sma' hours in his Fifth Avenue home – they would talk, like all Scots abroad, about the old home town and the Highlands – Andrew Carnegie wrote out letters of introduction for Harry to friends and colleagues right across the Continent.

Lauder was greatly impressed by Carnegie's politeness and kindliness, and by the patient way he had of arranging things for him. He realised he had a real friend at court in the Scots-born steel magnate. The two men admired each other's shrewdness and efficiency, the product, no doubt, of the background of early struggle and hardship which had been the boyhood lot of them both.

Carnegie and Lauder were both small in stature, and had many a laugh as they argued out who was the smaller. One evening, in Harry's New York theatre, they settled it once and for all by comparing their respective heights against the dressing-room door. Lauder's manager, Tom Vallance, was called in as the referee, and declared that Carnegie was the taller by one-tenth of an inch.

The steel magnate had offered to give the comedian a useful tip on the stock exchange if he beat him. As he left the room, he pulled Harry aside and whispered in his ear: 'Buy United States Steel Commons.'

Next morning Lauder bought a thousand at thirty-two dollars. They simply rocketed over the next few months, but, alas, Harry, the canny Scot, had sold his lot before they reached the topmost price. Otherwise, he might have made a small fortune – thanks to the confidential tip he got from Andrew Carnegie.

Another good friend of Harry Lauder was Sir Thomas Lipton, the grocer laddie from Glasgow, who rose to be a millionaire through dint of hard work and sweat, and built himself a grocery empire. Twenty years Lauder's senior, Lipton was of Irish parentage, and had worked in his teens in the USA as a clerk and a street-car driver.

That fateful New Year's Day of 1917 brings in a very human story connected with Lipton, a man Lauder admired for his successful life after early handicaps not unlike his own. Harry had spent that New Year's Eve, somewhat sadly, in the Clapham, London, home of his manager and brother-in-law, Tom Vallance, but his thoughts had been far away with his son at the battlefront in France. He had an awful foreboding of tragedy.

Returning early to his hotel in Bloomsbury, after deciding not to celebrate the arrival of New Year, he found a message at the porter's desk.

'Sir Thomas Lipton rang up to speak to you,' Lauder was told. 'He said he would like to talk with you when you come in.'

It was half an hour before midnight, and Harry called up his friend at his home. There was a slight halt in Lipton's conversation when they were connected, and it seemed as if Sir Thomas was waiting to hear something.

'Oh, Harry, I . . . I only wanted to wish you a Happy New Year,' he said. 'When it comes, of course. It's still 1916. There are still a few minutes of the Old Year to go.'

Then Lipton enquired how Mrs Lauder was, and rang off, saying: 'Well, Harry, I just wanted to have a wee talk with you before the bells ring in 1917. See and get yourself a good night's sleep. And a Guid New Year when it comes. Goodnight to you, Harry'.

Sir Thomas rang off, and Lauder went to bed. It wasn't until next day, when the telegram arrived telling him officially of his son's death at the front, that he learned why Lipton had made that end-of-the-year telephone call. He had already been informed of Captain John Lauder's death, and had called up Harry to pass on his regrets and sympathy. Then, realising that Harry was without official word, he found it the kind of bad news he couldn't give a friend at a moment in time when the rest of the world was preparing to celebrate the arrival of a New Year. He had rung off, knowing that bad news would be easier to break in the light of daytime.

Will Fyffe, the late and great Scottish character comedian, who gave the world his immortal song *I Belong To Glasgow* (although he really hailed from Dundee), was another close friend of Harry Lauder. Fyffe came on the showbusiness scene at a later stage than Lauder. He was seventeen years his junior, and must have been touring around the old-style drama fit-ups in the early 1900s at about the time Harry Lauder was planning his assault on the London music-hall.

Early in his career, Will heard of Lauder, introduced himself, and offered Harry some Scottish character sketches. Alas, Harry didn't see them fitting his own style, and he promptly returned them. According to many reliable sources, Fyffe had songs to sell because he needed the money badly, and one of those he offered to Harry Lauder was *I'm Ninety-Four Today*, which later became one of his classics.

More intriguing, however, is the story – a true one, as I know – that he offered Harry another song called *I Belong To Glasgow*, and Lauder also tossed that one back at him as being 'unsuitable'. It is interesting now to reflect how music-hall fame might have been changed for Harry (and for Fyffe, too) if he had accepted the Glasgow song.

Would he have gone on to make it as world famous as Will Fyffe did? And would Will Fyffe have found a substitute for the number that later became his password in variety tours all round the world? The answer is anybody's guess. But I know Harry Lauder always had memories of that song whenever it was sung in his hearing. It isn't every day that you get the chance of buying a potential song-hit for a matter of a few pounds!

Sir Harry Lauder and his secretary-companion, his niece Greta, were often in the audiences to enjoy Will Fyffe in pantomime at the Theatre Royal and Alhambra in Glasgow. On these occasions word would be sent round to Fyffe, and sometimes he worked in a gag about his distinguished visitor.

In the pantomime *The King And Queen Of Hearts*, playing the role of the king, Will would find himself in need of gold, and would suddenly lift a stage telephone and call up Lauder Ha'. The audience would hear him recount his plight to Sir Harry, ostensibly at the other end of the line, and ask for his financial aid.

Then Fyffe would replace the receiver, face the audience with the most crestfallen look he could assume, and tell them: 'Nae luck – Harry says he hasn't worked for ten years!' It always brought a huge laugh, especially from Lauder and his niece.

The two stars were friends for many years and enjoyed many a good conversation about America and the British music-hall. They often talked about starring together; one of their ideas was to present the drama *Rob Roy*, with Fyffe as Rob Roy and Harry cast as Bailie Nicol Jarvie.

If that project had ever come to fruition, it would surely have made theatre history. Harry Lauder and Will Fyffe as co-stars was surely a combination that would have packed any theatre for many years.

People in showbusiness make many friends. The alleged glamour of the stage and life behind the footlights attracts all types of people round to the colourful but often frenetic world of backstage life. They range from genuine fans and admirers to what some in theatre business call 'the hangers-on'.

Harry Lauder had more admirers than cadgers among his friends. More important, however, he became himself a great fan of other stars whom he genuinely admired. This unselfish trend was noticeable all through his life. He certainly had no rivals in his own particular field, but he never envied the fame and glory that came to other stars among his contemporaries. He had a considerable confidence in his own talent, and no fear of being outstripped in the race to the top.

I think one of the most memorable moments was to find 'wee

Harry' going round backstage in a Glasgow theatre to pay due homage to that great Hollywood couple of slapstick and mime, Stan Laurel and Oliver Hardy. He sat through their show, and when the curtain fell, went round, as was his custom, to thank them for providing him – and their audience – with so entertaining an act.

In Balmoral bonnet and kilt, Lauder trekked through the pass-door with his niece, Miss Greta, to pay his respects to the American comedians. He was welcomed to their dressing-room immediately, for the word had got around that the 'great Sir Harry Lauder' was coming to see them and pay his respects. There wasn't an American artiste that came to Britain who hadn't heard of Harry Lauder.

Stan Laurel and Ollie Hardy were thrilled, of course. Stan Laurel himself had close family associations with the old Scotia Music-hall in Glasgow where Harry had entertained in his youth. They had much to talk over.

Lauder always remembered what it was like for a 'foreigner' to tour another country. He remembered what it meant to have an established performer in the States pop round backstage in Chicago or Los Angeles or New York, and comment favourably on the act. Little words of praise, he realised, meant so much when you were on tour.

I always remember him laughing heartily with Laurel and Hardy, shaking hands with them, inviting them to his home, and leaving with a chuckle and the quite unnecessary (in their case) quip and advice: 'Remember, lads, keep your stuff clean . . . keep it clean!'

There is a story that, when he visited Laurel and Hardy, he sat for an hour on a dressing-basket in their room, and sang chorus after chorus of his songs. It may well have happened, and I'm sure it did, but I can't vouch for the truth of that story.

Harry Lauder loved meeting American stars on his own home territory. In a way, he felt they were doing exactly what he had done years before in their own land, and now they were repaying the courtesy with a tour of their own. The United Kingdom being a much smaller territory, it was all on a far smaller scale, of course.

Charlie Chaplin was one of Lauder's greatest chums. He met him several times on his visits to California, and was always invited to see round the film studios with him in Hollywood. Harry and Charlie enjoyed many a good 'crack' together, as Scotsmen call a conversation of real warmth and recollection. They talked over the old days when Charlie was on the British music-hall stage.

And hadn't Chaplin played Glasgow, too? Harry said he remembered him in Britain from his days as a member of Fred Karno's company. He didn't know him by name then, but he used to leave the stage, go round to the front of the theatre, and laugh right merrily at this black-haired lad with the red-red nose and the 'wobbly-body' movements.

Whenever his tour hit California, Chaplin, in turn, made a point of being in one of the audiences to watch Lauder; they struck up a strong mutual admiration for each other's so-contrasting talents in comedy and song. Harry Lauder, aspiring towards perfection in gesture and movement, could never see enough of the Chaplin gift for mime. Both were little men in height (though so great in star stature), and both had come up from poor working class backgrounds. And both, surprisingly, had played the dear old Argyle Theatre in Birkenhead within months of each other.

Harry Lauder, regular visitor to America, came to be on first-name terms with many of the 'greats' of the Hollywood motion picture screen. This came about through his frequent visits to America, during which his touring one-man show always touched on sunny California.

At the studios he met Mary Pickford, Harold Lloyd, Gloria Swanson, Bessie Love, Douglas Fairbanks senior, John Gilbert and many more. All of them were delighted to meet up with this 'cute li'l Skatsman' from Glasgow, and to hear the healthy burr-r-r in his voice.

Lauder loved the atmosphere of Hollywood at that time, the hard work the movie actors put in, and the gay and warmhearted folk so many of them turned out to be. He was always impressed by their so-serious attitude to work and the manner in which they completely forgot about it once they were off the set.

In later years Harry got to know American stars like Bob Hope, Bing Crosby, Danny Kaye and many more. The expertise and efficiency of most American stars always impressed him, and he knew that this was, so often, the secret of their international success. Lauder appreciated that, to achieve anything worthwhile amid the bright lights, a performer had to work tirelessly on improvements to his or her act, adding a little extra here and a little bit there. He was a true admirer of the American 'know-how'.

Harry came too early in life for the heyday of the talking-picture. Had movies with speech been introduced earlier in the century, he might well have moved into this medium, although, in all truth, it was the warm and intimate 'feel' of a real live audience he preferred.

Nevertheless, at a fairly early stage in his career – as early as 1907, it is said by some – he had made a few short song films for the Gaumont company in Britain, and he is even reputed to have been paid well into four figures for making these. It wasn't until he was close to his sixtieth birthday, however, that Lauder was offered important film parts.

By 1930 the talkies had arrived in Britain, and astute producers immediately thought of the magic of his name up there in lights above the world's movie theatres. He was offered a number of different roles, and in 1930 signed a contract to make several films. He did several, the only important one being *Huntingtower*. He often mentioned the discomfort it caused. For this film he had to climb up and down cliffs, and was soaked with salt sea-water spray. It was exacting work.

At heart, Harry disliked intensely the upsets that film-making brought in those early days, the impersonal feeling a camera caused, and the thick and heavy make-up that was considered necessary for an actor. Being at the beck and call of an often temperamental film director was another hazard.

Radio, however, was a completely different medium, and one in which he was starting to shine. Harry went to the BBC studio microphone in the Savoy Hill days, and managed to put over his warm personality to the person listening at home in Britain on those early (and now so primitive-looking) sets. The producers of 'the wireless', as it was commonly called, valued his services.

When he did a broadcast at Christmas in 1925, he was given the highest fee ever paid at that time by the British Broadcasting Corporation. It was in the region of £1,500.

Harry admitted, like so many broadcasters, to having 'mike-fright', but he always came across well, and used to visualise thousands of little scattered groups lying listening to him in homes and hospitals up and down the country.

A Harry Lauder show on 'the wireless' was a big event in any year. People looked forward to it for days, if not weeks, in advance. I used to tune-in myself on primitive earphones as a schoolboy around 1928, when Harry went through a wide reper-toire of his songs. It was one of the entertainment events of the year, especially for listeners in isolated and rural areas of Britain. Lauder himself was a keen radio listener, a real addict of 'the wireless'.

Surprisingly for a Scotsman of his time, he was a campaigner for brighter fare on radio on Sundays. He used to argue that the type of dull programme offered by the BBC on a Sunday 'only tempts us to tune-in to the wicked Continent'.

Lauder remained a popular broadcasting artiste even in the eventide of his life, when he used to take part in radio programmes from the BBC studios in Glasgow. Luckily, some of these shows have been preserved for all time in the sound archives of the BBC, and excerpts from them are still heard from time to time.

At the studios in Glasgow Sir Harry became a good friend of the conductor of the BBC Scottish Orchestra, the late Ian Whyte, and often broadcast with his orchestra. Another associate in radio was Howard M Lockhart, the well-known Scottish broadcaster, who used to be variety producer for the BBC at Glasgow.

One is tempted to wonder today how Harry Lauder would have fitted into the medium of television. Would he have relegated it into the impersonal, electronic category? Or would he have welcomed it as a way of getting across with warmth and personality to millions? Personally, I think Harry Lauder would have proved quite a personality on television, especially in colour. He would have become an annual event as the star of round-the-world programmes on New Year's Eve.

What a fabulous audience of many nations he might have enjoyed if he had been born into an age of global television! Producers could have linked him from a studio in his native Scotland by satellite to many millions of homes all round the earth. *The Ed Sullivan Show* and *The Hollywood Palace* would surely have taken second place then to *The Harry Lauder Show*, in 'glorious tartan-colour'.

But then we're not all fortunate enough to be in the right spot at the right time. Lauder, who belonged to the age of British music-hall and the heyday of American vaudeville, didn't live to enjoy the great home luxury of television-style entertainment, either in black-and-white or in colour. He would, I know for sure, have been one of its greatest supporters. That Lauder kilt and tartan – and that magic voice and chuckle – would have come over with great richness and warmth.

Before colour television and radio, the gramophone-playing cult enjoyed a boom, and millions of people in many countries were regular buyers of the jaunty songs of Harry Lauder in the form of the old-style 78-revolutions-per-minute records.

Some of these old recordings are collectors' pieces today. Great is the joy of a knowledgeable collector who browses through the antique shops or the junk-stores – in London, New York or Glasgow – and suddenly comes on a record by Harry Lauder.

Several Lauder '78s' have a real historical value because, in the first instance, not too many of them were pressed. They rank with similar thick and heavy brittle discs by stars like Florrie Forde, Marie Lloyd, Little Tich or George Robey. I've known really enthusiastic record collectors and music-hall fans to pay as much as thirty dollars for one such rare '78'.

Early recordings by Harry Lauder were made on the old-style cylindrical records, neatly packaged inside cylinders, and played on the old-fashioned machines, turned with the hand by means of a handle.

After his great success with the song *I Love A Lassie* in the Glasgow Theatre Royal pantomime of Christmas 1905, Lauder found himself in demand to make records. This was a fairly new 'toy' for home entertainment, but it was the fashionable thing to own a gramophone, and to invite your friends to your home to hear the latest song-hits from London town. The bigger the gramophone-recording star, the more friends you amassed!

Harry Lauder often regretted, in later years, that he made some of his first recordings for so small a fee. The trouble was that it all sounded so easy, and took up so little of his time. But he realised later on that he had been foolhardy to make these recordings so cheaply.

He always maintained that the Gramophone Company of Great Britain pulled one of their cleverest deals when they signed him up almost literally 'for a song'. The routine was that the artiste popped into the studios, and made about half a dozen records in the one day for a pound a song. If the artiste could offer the producer six songs, then he walked out with a fiver on the spot.

For such small fees as this, Harry Lauder made his very first recordings of popular songs like *She's Ma Daisy*, *Stop Yer Tickling*, *Jock!*, *Tobermory*, and that early music-hall number about the tailor, *Calligan, Call Again!*

Still, who can blame an artiste at the start of a career? Five pounds was still, at that time, 'big money' to a man like Lauder. In the mines he would have had to work for a fortnight for that kind of return. Besides, the men who made these early recordings were not offering any more.

But his name and growing fame spelt a goldmine for the early gramophone recording tycoons, and soon his records were being snatched up in both Britain and America. In the years that followed, millions, literally, of Harry Lauder records were to sell wherever his name was known, and that was just about everywhere.

The type of early phonograph which brought the cheerful Lauder voice, melodies and chuckle into so many homes in the first two decades of this century can still be seen, and played, in the museums of Britain. One that belonged to Harry Lauder himself occupied an honoured place for years in the Curio Room at Lauder Ha', where visitors were invited to turn the handle and listen again to the rough early reproductions of the cylinders. This primitive machine was bought at the Lauder Ha' auction by Jimmy Logan, the Scottish theatre-owner, and has gone into his collection of early music-hall relics.

Harry Lauder often had his regrets about his incursion into the gramophone-recording business, with all its royalty ramifications. He used to sit back sometimes and think of all the money he ought to have made from their widespread sales across the globe.

'And to think I signed mysel' away for a mere five pounds once!' he used to say. 'I should rightly have been worth a hundred times that sum.

'Caruso and I had once a wee crack about this, and he fair made me envious with talk of the royalties his records brought him. It made me realise how rash I'd been to sign mysel' away for a pound a song.'

Caruso, Lauder and Melba were the big sellers among the recordings of their time, and became real Top of the Pops long before anyone had ever thought of inventing a chart to record who was at the top each week.

Lauder's later relations with the recording companies were more cordial, however, and he stayed at the top of the charts for close on two decades, something that the present-day disc personalities, gliding up and down the lists like yo-yos, could never imagine possible.

If you should chance at any time on one of the original Harry Lauder recordings, be sure to guard it well. As recording techniques improve and develop, these old 78 rpm records take on a new value because of their historical appeal.

Before me, as I write, is one of my own personal collection, a Zonophone Celebrity Record, with its red label. Well-worn, it looks as if it has been played many thousands of times on the old-fashioned gramophone. The label gives the singer the designation 'Scottish Comedian', and announces *A Wee Hoose 'Mang The*

Heather, written by Lauder and Elton, on the one side, and that great old favourite, *She's The Lass For Me*, a Lauder composition, on the other.

From songs and recordings like these, played from country cottage to royal palace, Scotland's grandeur once sprang, thanks to the ex-pitboy singer and a simple machine you wound up to full strength by physically turning a handle.

Harry Lauder was, indeed, the Top of the Pops for millions. And the royalties for his songs and recordings are still flowing in steadily to his family trust in the heart of modern Scotland.

Royal Summons from the Bath

HARRY LAUDER WAS a good friend of the ordinary man-in-the-street, be it in New York or London, Melbourne or Glasgow. He was also a genuine friend of kings and queens. There was no snobbery. British royalty took to him like a brother.

It was, I'm certain, the warmth and friendliness of the Scot's personality that did the trick. Lauder had the knack of piercing through the regalia and finding the essential human being underneath. In his career he often met the kings and queens of Britain, the princes and dukes and duchesses. British royalty has always been showbusiness conscious. They regularly went to the theatre to see Lauder perform, and, more than once, some of them would go backstage to have a chat with the ex-miner from the Scottish coalfields.

Harry was one of the acts chosen for the first-ever Royal Command Performance in British music-hall. It took place on the night of the 1st July 1912 at the Palace Theatre in London. Lauder found it a night to remember. On the bill with him was Harry Tate, the great English comedian from Birkenhead, who was offering his famous 'Motoring' sketch. Vesta Tilley, the male impersonator, and a real queen of the English music-hall, was also there, and so were George Robey, Wilkie Bard (the character comedian with the high forehead and longish hair), Clarice Mayne (that fine Principal Boy of pantomime), and Anna Pavlova, the great dancer of the ballet.

It was a night for all the 'greats' of the theatre profession. Harry

Lauder had the difficult task of following Pavlova and members of the Imperial Russian Ballet. It was a challenge that he accepted, and he stayed on to conquer the distinguished London audience, singing his number *Roamin' In The Gloamin'*, which he had introduced only eighteen months before in pantomime at the Theatre Royal in Glasgow; the song was then at the very height of its popularity.

That first Royal Command Performance at the theatre in London's Shaftesbury Avenue set the seal on Lauder's fame. The audience was composed of the richest and most elegant people of the era, for the show was an official Command show. Present-day royal shows are not strictly Command shows, but merely Royal Variety Performances.

This show of July 1912 was unique in that a direct individual approach was made by royalty to the artistes taking part. In the royal shows since then, impresarios or organisations are invited to put on a special performance and to select the artistes taking part. There is a genuine difference; royal shows today are incorrectly described as 'Command Performances'.

Strictly speaking, however, the show at the London Palace was not the first time Lauder had been commanded to entertain his king.

An earlier event took place at Rufford Abbey in 1909. Lauder was then appearing in music-hall at the old Paragon Theatre in the Mile End Road, London. One night a letter was delivered to him. It came from the King's private secretary, and it commanded him to sing before the monarch, then King Edward the Seventh, at the Abbey.

The King was on a visit to Lord and Lady Savile at Rufford, and it had been put to him that he might like to have an entertainment from a leading British performer. King Edward the Seventh didn't take long to decide who he should ask. 'Tell Harry Lauder to come up and sing for us,' he said.

Harry took his son John, then two months short of his six-teenth birthday, to play the piano for him. Father and son were given a warm welcome by Lady Savile, the hostess for the evening. Nervously, Harry handed over to her a list of the songs he proposed to sing, and Lady Savile, in turn, passed them on for King Edward's approval. The King was then sixty-eight years old, and he had been hearing many interesting reports of this Scots fellow Lauder and his triumphs across the Atlantic.

Back came the command from His Majesty that 'Mr Lauder should simply start at the top of his list of songs, and he would be told when to stop.'

It seemed as if all the society of England were present at that one-man concert in Rufford Abbey. About fifty or sixty notables were there, many house-party guests for the races at Doncaster.

The little 'stage' was set up in an underground vault of the castle, the King sitting near the front beside Lord and Lady Savile, while the lords and ladies, dukes and duchesses filled up the room along with all the servants at the Abbey.

Lauder opened his act with, of course, *I Love A Lassie*, and followed with favourites like *Tobermory*, *Stop Yer Ticklin', Jock!* and *We Parted On The Shore*.

He kept on singing, feeling half-way through, after half a dozen songs, that he would get the command to wind up the act. But there came no such royal instruction. So he kept right on to the end of his list of ten numbers.

Stepping forward, Harry announced: 'I'm sorry, your Majesty, lords and ladies, but I can sing no more tonight. And for a verra good reason. (He gave the famous Lauder chuckle.) You see, I've got nae mair music wi' me!'

Amid laughter and enthusiastic applause from his small but distinguished audience, Harry Lauder was given permission to withdraw, along with his son, and he dashed off to the room where he had dressed. He was hot and tired that warm September evening, and he decided to take a bath in the ante-room connected with his dressing-room. He was having a vigorous rub-down when a royal equerry came in to say that His Majesty wished to see him.

'Och, but no' like this!' joked the wee Scot. 'Ask him if he'd mind waitin' a wee meenit or twa. I'll no' be long.'

The equerry said he would convey the message back to the King, and that he would doubtless wait for him. Harry Lauder put that incident high on his list of Great Moments. He often joked about it in later years.

'Imagine it!' he told me. 'I can cross my heart and honestly say I'm one of the verra few men in the world who ever kept a king waiting!'

But he wasn't long in leaping out of that bath in Rufford Abbey. He was dressed and smartened-up in a couple of minutes, and soon was making his bow before the King, who told him how much he had enjoyed the act.

'Aye, I'm thinking you surely must have done,' said Harry. 'Otherwise, your Majesty, I wouldna' hae run oot o' sangs tae sing tae ye!'

Harry Lauder was often summoned to sing at private house parties in mansions, castles and palaces. On another occasion, in 1924, he was invited to give a special performance before King George the Fifth and Queen Mary at Balmoral Castle, in the north-east of Scotland.

Lauder found himself on home-ground here, for he was in the Highlands, the area from where his dear mother Isabella MacLennan and her ancestors had come. The King and Queen showed much kindness to Sir Harry and Lady Lauder during this visit to Balmoral in 1924, and presented them with two framed photographs of themselves, suitably autographed. For years they adorned the top of Harry's piano.

Lauder always had a humorous remark or joke when he encountered Royalty. He was a master of the snappy and happy answer. Once he was entertaining at the Hippodrome Theatre in London when Royalty arrived to see his act in the person of the Prince of Wales, later the Duke of Windsor. The Prince and Harry liked each other immensely, Lauder appreciating particularly the Prince's complete lack of 'side' and swank.

Harry stopped in the middle of his patter, looked straight up at the royal box, fixed his eyes on the Prince, a most eligible bachelor then, and remarked: 'Aye, and I'm tellin' you, sir-r-r. A bonnie Scots lassie is the finest thing you can find on this earth. A man might dae worse.'

The Prince of Wales, applauding vigorously, called back: 'That's right, Harry. I might do worse.'

Then Lauder asked the house for requests. The Prince, in good form, called from his box: '*I Love A Lassie*, Harry. *I Love A Lassie*.' Quick as a flash, the Scots minstrel quipped back: 'Aye, we know you do, sir-r-r, but whit we a' want tae know is – *who is she?*' (saying it with a great happy Lauder chuckle). The house almost collapsed with laughter at this crack.

The Prince of Wales and Harry Lauder were obviously good friends, and Harry knew he could afford to joke with him like this. The audiences at the Hippodrome loved the cross-talk between Prince and music-hall star.

Probably the most amusing encounter with British royalty for Harry took place at the Palace Theatre when King George and Queen Mary came in one night specially to see the Lauder performance.

A well-known concert manager in London, George Ashton, was stage-managing the theatre visit for the King and Queen, and, at the interval, he went round to see Lauder and tell him that their Majesties would like to talk with him in the royal box.

Harry put on his tartan jacket, and went up immediately to see his King and Queen. The conversation became engrossing, since their Majesties had so many questions to ask him about his visits to America, his songs and patter, and where he got his ideas for the numbers.

Suddenly Harry had to leave, for the finale was almost due and all the artistes had to re-appear. He took his farewell of the King and Queen, and was in the corridor outside the royal box when he encountered the Duke of Connaught. George Ashton duly introduced Lauder and then moved off up the corridor himself.

'Richt, then, George, goodnight. And good luck!' Harry called out loudly to George Ashton as he left.

At that very moment King George the Fifth emerged from his theatre box into the corridor to stretch his legs, and heard the unmistakable Lauder farewell. He knew Harry was really talking to someone else, but he decided to make a joke out of it. A great big smile came over the King's face, and he turned in the direction of Lauder and cried out: 'And good nicht and good luck to you, too, Harry!'

That quick and humorous retort from his own monarch had poor Harry blushing all over – and completely floored. He feared for one awful moment that he might be taken up for treason, no less. Imagine calling your King by his first name! But King George the Fifth went off chuckling loudly, greatly amused at his own joke.

Harry often said he always went scarlet whenever he thought back to that incident at the Palace Theatre in London. But what a happy royal story to tell his friends and cronies in future years!

His links with society had a more realistic slant. Early in this century, Lauder realised the appeal that he, a comical Scotsman, had for the titled folk of London, and he made many a good bargain with them in connection with private shows.

These were really one-man cabaret performances. Harry would stage them in the drawing-rooms of the big houses in the West End of London, where the cream of the metropolitan society came to be entertained, and stayed to admire and applaud.

For these evenings with the dukes and duchesses, Harry didn't try to smarten-up his song-and-comedy act, or even attempt to make it more sophisticated. In fact, it was the simple and homely song that registered most at these late-evening cabarets. The favourite number with London's fashionable set was always *I Love A Lassie*; they even joined in the choruses.

Lauder now made sure he got full recompense for the good value he gave. A regular fee for such concerts was £110. All it involved was a show lasting, probably, forty-five minutes in one of the big swanky homes in Kensington or Belgravia. It was worth the journey from the music-hall to well-paid 'wee jobs' like these.

Such midnight engagements with the society folk of London helped to compensate poor Harry for the mere ten pounds he was probably earning for the entire week's appearance at the Tivoli in the Strand or some other music-hall. Lauder even toured three or four suburban variety halls in the same evening, his manager, Tom Vallance, driving him between them in Harry's very first motor-car.

Harry often squirmed when he thought of these early contracts he had signed himself away with. He made up his mind that, one day, he would gain his own back and extract every pound possible from managements who had held him to such poor figures while he made hundreds for them at every performance.

Some years later a London theatre owner almost went down on his knees begging Harry Lauder to play for him. Harry remembered him as one of the managers who had kept him pegged to a meagre fee, and asked his agent to quote him a fee of £400 a week. The theatre owner almost fainted at the mention of such a figure, and suggested that Lauder could reduce this to something more realistic.

'Aye, then,' said Harry, 'tell him I'll come down to £450. An' if he disnae like that, my next cut will be down to £500.'

The manager in question could take the Lauder bargaining no longer. He sent round the £400 contract post-haste within half an hour.

What a contrast was the generosity of theatre managements in the United States of America! Not only did they talk in terms of thousands, but they were also ready and willing to buy out Harry's old contracts in London theatres so that he could more quickly work for them. Managements like these in New York, Chicago and Philadelphia were realising the true worth of the tartan minstrel.

It wasn't that Harry Lauder had any big-headed notions about himself. He simply realised that his flair for song and humour was a gift he had – one given him by God, he often said – and that it could attract thousands of people to pay over good, hard-earned money to see him. He saw no reason why he, a hard-headed Scot who had once been 'stung' in London, shouldn't share in much of the profit from his gift.

He realised that it was no use for anybody to act the jester before the world if he wasn't going to be well rewarded for the job. Lauder became a good bargainer, and he earned a fortune as a result. This, in a way, was justice because when he first hit the jackpot in the London music-hall in the springtime of 1900, he signed his name to contracts that tied him down to a small salary. It was a rash move, as he realised within a few years, and he determined there and then that he would never become an 'easy-contract victim' again.

The truth was that he committed himself to appear in London halls for fairly small salaries, despite the fact that the audiences were going deliriously wild with delight over his entertainment potential.

'Aye, man, I was too impetuous,' he used to say, years afterwards. 'A fool, indeed. I signed away my name to contracts, being so happy then just to get into the London scene.

'Later on I discovered other performers were away down the bill, and they were getting four or five times as much as yours truly. And me, Harry Lauder, the man whose name was pulling in the customers. I'm tellin' you, I was richt daft.

'I used to go out into some of the provincial halls in the north, after London, and earn the real money I was due.'

Caught up in a net of cheap contracts in London town, Harry Lauder nevertheless was as good as his word, and never let a management down. He honoured every signature, and was only absent when his American agent bought out his contract from certain managements so that he could continue working in the land of the almighty dollar.

This early financial experience taught Harry a true lesson. It made him all the more shrewd and careful when signing for future engagements. It also gave him a strong bargaining sense in dealing with agents and managers.

All through his career Harry retained this sense, and was alert not to sign himself away for a pittance of what he was worth. He had a great faith in his own talents and knew that he was a 'draw' at the box-office. He made up his mind that he would never again see other artistes on the same bill earning more money than himself.

Request from Winston Churchill

As if one world war hadn't been enough, along came a second, and once again Harry Lauder the entertainer was in there pitchin' – ready to do his duty for his king and country.

'If I can hirple on to the platform and sing a wee song, it shall be my duty to do so,' he said, at the outset of hostilities. And he kept his promise.

Not so active naturally – he was now approaching his seventieth birthday – the little minstrel from Lauder Ha' made public appearances whenever he could to help raise money for war charities, or to entertain lonely or homesick Servicemen.

With the war only a few weeks old, we find him giving a concert to the troops in the blackout on an October night in 1939, and singing a new song, *Pin Your Faith On The Motherland*. There were to be many more such concerts, and Lauder was at most of them. He became a special favourite with the American troops who came over to Scotland, and were billeted around Glasgow and the west. Many had heard from their own fathers of how good an ambassador for Britain this man Lauder had been in the previous great war in Europe.

So it was natural that, when she visited Scotland in November 1942, Mrs Eleanor Roosevelt should ask specially to meet Sir Harry. They got together at a luncheon in Glasgow after Mrs Roosevelt had toured the Clydeside shipyards. It was Harry Lauder, in fact, who led the farewell chorus to her of *Will Ye No' Come Back Again?*

Back home in America, Mrs Roosevelt went to the microphone and told the nation later that same month: 'People like Sir Harry Lauder, who devotes many an evening to the entertainment of our boys in the Glasgow American Red Cross Club, are adding day by day to the good feeling which must inevitably exist between us.'

Sir Harry spent the war years based on his home on the Lanarkshire moors, south of Glasgow, and many an evening he would be driven home just as the Nazi bombers were being spotted in the skies above, desperately trying to reach the naval bases in the west and the dockland area around Glasgow and the Clyde. He was at his Lauder Ha' home on that disastrous night in March 1941 when the German raiders let loose their bombs on the industrial and shipyard town of Clydebank, and left heavy devastation and death in their wake.

Lauder passionately hated war, and he had taken his full share of its effects. Now he had the greatest sympathy with men and women who were losing their own loved ones in a second European conflagration.

If he ruled the world, he once said, he would never allow people 'to be so daft as to fill battlefields with twisted dead and homes with sobbing women.'

It was all of a quarter of a century since his own son John had been killed at the front, and he never forgot that deep personal blow. It was enough to stop the Harry Lauder songs for all time. But there was a war to be fought, work to be done, and the great tartan trouper was ready at a moment's notice to play his part in keeping up a nation's morale. He toured extensively and gave concerts, and was regularly heard over the radio in special broadcasts to the nation and the men at the front.

Winston Churchill, leading Britain through and out of the storm, was one of Harry's wartime buddies, and they often exchanged notes and messages.

When the fighting was over there came a memorable day for Harry. The city of Edinburgh presented the Freedom of the Scottish capital to Winston Churchill for his services in war leadership.

'Please arrange to have Sir Harry Lauder join me on the platform,' Churchill said, in a message to the civic authorities.

It was a proud moment for Lauder as he drove from Lauder Ha' to meet the great wartime leader near Edinburgh, and to see him being granted the same Freedom honour that he himself had been given exactly nineteen years before.

Very soon it became obvious why Churchill had asked for Lauder's company. He paid him sterling tribute in his speech, referred to him as 'this Grand Old Minstrel', and made public reference to his famous song that had inspired so many, *Keep Right On To The End Of The Road*.

The 'Grand Old Minstrel' took up the cue, started to sing that very song, and soon had the entire Usher Hall audience joining in with him as he sang. It was, in a sense, history repeating itself. This was exactly how his own Freedom ceremony had ended in that very same hall.

It was yet another memorable and magic moment in the Great Scot's career.

Sir Harry was a deeply religious Scot. The God-fearing family background in which he had been brought up in that house in seaside Portobello stayed with him for the rest of his life. He was a regular reader of The Bible, together with his equally religious wife, Nancy.

There are lots of stories about Lauder the man, and many have, quite naturally, been embellished with the passing years. But here is one that seems to summarise all that he was, as a good Scot and as a man, and much of what he stood for. By the time of the blitz during World War Two, Sir Harry had officially retired. But on this particular Sunday night, dark and blustery, with the blackout to add to the inconvenience and danger of moving around in Britain, he remembered the hardships the boys at the front were suffering and agreed to make an appearance at the King's Theatre in Glasgow on behalf of a Red Cross charity.

He was driven out from his home on the moors above Strathaven into the chilly evening and to the city. An audience awaited and Lauder was expected to attend. When his act was announced, the sturdy wee Scot marched right down to the centre of the stage. How that Sunday night audience cheered! One man in the circle called out for *I Love A Lassie*. Another shouted for *Roamin' In The Gloamin'*. The cries were heard from all corners of the theatre.

There was a pause. A moment's hush. Solemnly, Lauder held up his hand, and the crowded audience immediately fell silent. Another meaningful pause. Then, quietly, Sir Harry started to speak.

'Ladies and gentlemen,' he said, 'this is the Sabbath day. A time to be serious. So, for tonight, we'll forget your requests, and I'll give you one song that is just right for this day. Please listen to me.'

Then, instead of singing one of his favourites, the little kilted knight sang in his rich strong voice the age-old song of faith and trust, *Rocked In The Cradle Of The Deep*.

And everyone present, young and old, joined in as he sang

> Secure I rest upon the wave,
> For Thou, O Lord, hast power to save,
> And calm and peaceful is my sleep,
> Rocked in the Cradle of the Deep . . .

If Harry Lauder hadn't decided to become an entertainer on the stage, what would he have done in his life's work? He often said he would have chosen to be a great writer, 'earning a shilling a word'. Or, maybe, a sailor, journeying to faraway and romantic places.

Or he might have chosen to be a minister in the Scottish High lands, living in a manse in a bonnie Highland glen. That way, he would have been able to prepare his sermons on a sunny lawn and to have had 'an audience every Sunday morning'.

Harry Lauder loved simple things . . . home, family, pets, a warm fire glowing in the hearth, good books, conversation, tasty dishes. He liked to be comfortable in his own home, often wearing a cosy tartan smoking-jacket. Off the stage, he was rarely seen without his beloved pipe. He liked to smoke – and think. He wore gold-rimmed spectacles, and he read a great deal. He built up a library of many books, lots of them about Scotland. There were volumes of songs of Scotland, and here and there you would find a book about a famous explorer like David Livingstone, or a book on the Scottish Covenanters.

Harry Lauder had a weakness for good wholesome love stories. This was natural for a singer who based so many of his ballads on the universal love theme, with bold laddies falling in love with bonnie, bonnie lassies. He kept dozens of little notebooks in his bedroom and his study. Into these he would pencil little poems and verses, and ideas for new songs. He was a great one for scribbling little notes and reminders when inspiration came along.

Reading the poems of Robert Burns, the Scottish poet, was one of his regular habits. He was an ardent admirer of the Ayrshire poet and shared his liking for verse about bonnie Scots lassies. Harry became, in later life, a keen collector of artistic things, and brought home much fine ivory and other work by oriental artists from his tours in the East.

People who asked him to list his outdoor interests were always given the same three answers: 'Tryin' tae hit a wee gutty ba''; 'Tryin' tae catch salmon and trout'; and 'Shootin''. Of the three, Lauder was keenest, like so many stage comedians, on the gentle art of angling. He liked to disappear into the Highlands of Scotland with his favourite rod and line.

He liked a casual style of dress, but the Scottish kilt was his preference on ninety per cent of outdoor occasions. It was very rarely that he was ever seen wearing trousers. He liked bright colourings, and was sometimes seen sporting a bright American tie 'monstrosity' – that's what the family called it – with the tartan of his MacLennan forebears.

The gay and sentimental Christmas season was the time of year he liked best. It was the time for talk with friends and relatives, and for enjoying your home. Every December the greetings started to arrive, piling up at his Scottish home and bringing him hours of memories as he remembered the senders in many far-flung corners of the world.

Big houses or little houses, all were home to Harry Lauder. He looked on home and fireside as the happiest and most desirable things in life. Always, he kept an affectionate spot in his heart for his very first 'but and ben', the wee house at Number Three Bridge Street in Portobello where he spent his first boyhood years. He was so proud of it he used to drive back to it in his golden years, stop his Rolls-Royce outside, and proudly show it off to his friends.

Lauder was as proud of that 'wee hoosie' in Portobello, near the sea, as he became in later life of his grand mansion on the moors. Both represented home and loved ones to him, and that was all that mattered.

But Harry also loved his first home as a young married man in that miners' row in Hamilton, just as he loved the villa that

143

became his working base in Tooting, London, and his Laudervale house close to his beloved Firth of Clyde at Dunoon.

Home was where Lauder's heart was, like the hearts of so many Scots. And home came into many of his most popular songs. He loved to talk and sing of the kettle 'singing' on the fire, or of a bonnie vista of someone's cottage home in the West Highlands, or of an old cabin home by the sea.

Wherever he travelled, Lauder liked to pick up an article as a souvenir to take home. He collected many items from many countries for each room in his house. There were so many in the end that they overflowed into his Curio Room at Lauder Ha'. Many were gifts, passed on to him by enthusiastic admirers.

A walk around any of Harry's homes became like a conducted tour of the world. Something was always being pointed out that had come from a distant land or city. He was especially proud of the parquet flooring in the study of his home at Laudervale, in Dunoon. It was of mahogany which had come from the Philippines, and which he had brought home along with him. His home at Lauder Ha', amid the hills of Scotland, was similarly filled with little things that meant so much from his travels.

There have been arguments about Harry's actual birthplace in Portobello in 1870. Some say that Number Three Bridge Street was not his birthplace, and that he was, in fact, born in a little house in Bridge Street Lane. This ran between Bridge Street and Pipe Street, and was demolished as derelict property many years ago.

The evidence in favour of the argument is the surgery record-book of the doctor who brought Harry into the world. The surgeon's grandson corroborated it in later years. If this story is correct, it would seem that, after his birth in Bridge Street Lane, the baby Harry was carried round to his grandparents' home in

Bridge Street, which was larger, and that he stayed there for some time.

Shortly before the 1914–18 war, Harry, already a fairly rich man through his long, record-breaking American tours, invested in the estate of Glen Branter, near Dunoon, in the West Highlands of Scotland. The house here was quite a mansion, with turrets that made him feel he had bought a castle. It stood on the shores of Loch Eck, and Harry planned to build a house in the grounds for his son John, who was studying for a career as a barrister. John was engaged to be married to his boyhood sweetheart, Mildred Thomson, the pretty daughter of a London merchant, Robert Thomson.

The Glen Branter estate was a picturesque spot, much loved by Harry and Nance, and their son. It had some fine stretches of river fishing, and Loch Eck itself was always good for a catch.

The Lauders adored 'The Glen', as they called it, with its wonderful views of Scottish mountains, its wild life, and its fine larch trees and shrubs. But Harry didn't prove a very prosperous farmer or Highland laird, and he lost a considerable amount of money in the fluctuating fortunes of owning sheep and cattle, and planting trees. Improvements to the house and estate cost a small fortune.

The final blow came with the death of his son John at the front during the Great War. Glen Branter held too many memories of John for both Harry and Nance, and they sold the estate to the Forestry Commission, which was taking over the glen for afforestation. Harry and Nance, however, were still to have a number of happy years together in their home by the Firth of Clyde at Dunoon.

Memories of the Lauders remain in Glen Branter to the present day. Lady Lauder is buried there; she lies close to a red stone monument on a little knoll on the north side of the main road from Dunoon to Strachur. Harry and Nance set up this monument after the 1914–18 war to the memory of their dear beloved son John, and were careful to leave enough room for a grave on either side for themselves.

When she died in 1927, Lady Lauder was buried on the right-hand side of the monument, and Sir Harry said that when his own time arrived he would go to rest here on the top of the wee hill in Glen Branter. As events turned out, he was buried beside his own family in the cemetery at Hamilton, Lanarkshire. But his spirit, I'm certain, soon found its way up to that lovely West Highland glen beside the lassie he loved most dearly.

After Harry sold his Glen Branter mansion, he made Laudervale in Dunoon his only home for a number of years. This house by the Clyde later became a hotel, and was eventually destroyed in a fire; its site is still pointed out by holiday guides to interested coach parties.

Then, in the mid-1930s, when his brother Alick died, Harry moved nearer to Glasgow, and settled in Lauder Ha', his last mansion home outside Strathaven (pronounced 'Strayven'), on the Lowland moors. With him went Alick's widow and her daughter Greta.

Lauder Ha' became a home that Harry loved. It overlooked the Covenanting country of southern Scotland and was steeped in Scottish history. The window in the hall bore the inscription that this house was the gift of God. From its windows there was a vista stretching over a radius of forty miles down to Tinto Hill and the rolling countryside of Dumfriesshire and the edge of the Scottish Borders.

As he neared the end of his great road through life, Sir Harry often strolled to the picture windows of his Lanarkshire home and looked out to the hills. In the evening he would sit by the fire and jot down stories and little snatches of songs in dozens of little notebooks. He remained a teller of stories and a writer of songs until near the end. The drawer in his bedroom dressing-table had several of these notebooks, filled with little bits of inspiration.

Lauder loved all his homes, and always looked forward to sailing back to Britain from overseas travels. A homecoming to family, friends and neighbours was one of his great joys. He loved travelling, but living out of a suitcase, as he said, was never quite as satisfying as the pleasures of unpacking it in the quiet of his own private abode by the shores of the Clyde.

Darlin' Greta

HIGH TEA IN Scotland on a late afternoon is a custom that few know much about today. In Harry Lauder's time it was almost a ritual, one that visitors to homes in country towns and cities came to appreciate to the full. It was the happiest part of many a day in homes all over Bonnie Scotland.

It meant a warm, welcoming fire in the hearth, and the tinkle of the silver spoons on the teacups and saucers as the trays and trolleys were wheeled in, laden with good home baking and cooking.

High tea or afternoon tea . . . it was always served with taste and delicacy at Lauder Ha'. This was his niece Greta's home as much as her uncle's. She brought the gentle, feminine touch to the place, just as Lady Lauder had done to previous Lauder family homes at Hamilton, Glasgow, Tooting and Dunoon during her lifetime.

With his wife gone, Harry had turned to his faithful niece, the girl who had accompanied him on so many tours and who knew his daily routine, his whims and little idiosyncrasies, as did nobody else. She was the daughter of his brother Alick Lauder, and what a help and Godsend she was to her famous uncle!

As Sir Harry said of her in the days when he lived by the Clyde at Dunoon, 'only her secret presence makes Laudervale, place of delightful ghosts and fragrant memories, still habitable for her lonely old uncle.'

When Sir Harry died in February 1950, Greta was determined

on one thing – that the name and fame of Harry Lauder should be kept alive in the big mansion house on the Lanarkshire moors. Nobody worked harder than Greta to keep the name of Lauder before the world, if indeed the world ever needed a reminder of so famous and distinguished a name.

So Lauder Ha' became a sort of proud memorial in the Scottish countryside to the minstrel who, for so long, had been a king in international showbusiness. His precious souvenirs of world travels were kept with loving care in the museum room that Harry had built up over the years. Proudly, they were on display, and shown to visitors and guests at Lauder Ha'. Even after Harry died, the trek of showbusiness personalities continued to this house of so many memories. It was a trek of faithful people who liked to know that they were either friends or ardent admirers of the Great Scot.

High tea and afternoon tea were still the custom, and it was an honour in Scotland to be invited to Lauder Ha'. Especially for the people of showbusiness who might be appearing at the big theatres in Glasgow, all less than an hour's drive away. Many of the great ones in showbusiness took the road out from Glasgow to the town of Strathaven. They usually made the trip after lunch, enjoyed high tea in the Lauder home, and drove back in early evening to be in time for curtain-up at the Empire or Alhambra theatres.

Sophie Tucker, Bob Hope, Maurice Chevalier, Bud Abbott and Lou Costello, Danny Kaye, Laurel and Hardy, Max Bygraves, Bruce Forsyth . . . the names were all there for the record in the distinguished visitors' book in that upstairs lounge at Lauder Ha'.

I made the journey myself many times after Sir Harry's death, taking the stars of the new and post-war showbusiness age to see the honoured home of a great international star of yesteryear. My wife and I had a standing arrangement with Greta that any stars we knew would be welcome at her home.

The lines carved on the interior of the hall at Lauder Ha' couldn't have put it more aptly or succinctly. They said, with that wonderful simplicity that was so much part of the Harry Lauder make-up:

> Frae ony airt the win' may blaw
> You're Welcome Here At Lauder Ha'

I remember well taking Bruce Forsyth, the famous English comedian, to see over Lauder Ha' and visit the trophy room where the mementoes and souvenirs of Sir Harry's world tours were so lovingly housed. Bruce, typical Londoner, and not even born when Harry Lauder was at his peak, nevertheless marvelled at what he saw.

'Marvellous . . . just marvellous!' was all he could say as Greta proudly conducted us on that well-routined tour of the great house and round the relics and souvenirs of many world tours.

On the drive back to Glasgow, Bruce Forsyth summed it all up. 'Marvellous! Simply marvellous!' he enthused. 'This man Lauder must have been a really Great Scot.'

Two nights later, back in London at the Palladium Theatre, Bruce told his nationwide audience of television millions about his visit to Scotland and his trip to the Harry Lauder home. As they watched *Sunday Night At The London Palladium* on their television set, Greta and her friends were just as thrilled at the reference as Bruce had been over his outing to Lauder Ha'. It was nice to be reassured that the world should still remember Sir Harry.

There were many other showbusiness visitors to Lauder Ha'. Morey Amsterdam, the Hollywood comedian, from *The Dick*

Van Dyke Show, went out with his wife Kay and son Gregory, and was equally thrilled; he shot many feet of film in and around the house and showed it later on television in America.

Greta Lauder – to her uncle she was always 'ma wee darlin' Greta' – brought a real queenly touch to life at Lauder Ha'. She was not only her uncle's constant companion after Lady Lauder died in 1927. She was also his secretary, manager and adviser. On their tours she played hostess to kings, queens, presidents and statesmen, and remained the same pleasant, modest and always-thoughtful Scots lass she had been since girlhood.

Life was always happy at Lauder Ha'. When friends called, and they were legion, especially in spring and summer, there was much conversation about life in Scotland and overseas. American accents mingled easily with Scots voices as old times and associations were recalled. Always – at the heart of the big house – there was Greta Lauder, herself so typically Scottish, so friendly and modest and at ease.

Showbusiness remained very much a part of Greta's life after her uncle's death. She was regularly seen as a first-nighter at the openings of the stage shows, big and small, in Glasgow, Edinburgh and Ayr. One of her great virtues was that she never ignored the little shows. It was in the wee revues, she always said, that the stars of tomorrow could be spotted.

Greta was nearly always accompanied by members of her own family, and regularly by her two nieces, Betty and Greta Fraser from Hamilton. The two young girls had been particular favourites of Sir Harry from girlhood days.

Often a whole row of front stalls was taken over by the Lauders from Lauder Ha' and Lanarkshire; they were great and keen theatregoers, and staunch supporters of the profession that Sir Harry had adorned so brilliantly. Greta – her full name was Margaret Horne Lauder – became a shrewd and capable judge of new talent, and often recommended an unknown artiste to the top producers and impresarios. She was an especially perceptive judge of Scottish comedy. It came naturally, no doubt, to someone who had been so closely associated with Scottish-style light entertainment all her life.

She regularly supported theatrical charities, and took a special interest in the Scottish Theatrical and Variety Artistes' Benevolent Fund, and in the Stars-for-Spastics shows in Glasgow and elsewhere.

As her uncle's secretary and concert manager, she was responsible for helping to arrange many entertainments for the troops given by Sir Harry during World War Two. How fitting it was, then, that she should be made a Member of the British Empire (MBE) in 1947, three years before Sir Harry's death.

Christmas time at Lauder Ha' had to be seen to be believed. Greta sent greetings and gifts to her friends all over the world, and from them, in many countries, the gifts and greetings came back by the hundred. There were festive baskets of glacé fruits, boxes of chocolates and more baskets of fresh fruit. Greta always sent them on to hospitals and children's homes, a gesture typical of her unselfish nature.

She had a warm spot in her heart for all who admired Sir Harry, as millions did. She once told me the story of how, one summer's day, a boy was seen sneaking up the driveway to Lauder Ha' and slipping behind a bush. Harry Lauder was relaxing in the sun. The family dog barked on hearing a movement in the drive. Greta went out to investigate, and spotted the lad.

The boy was taken aback, and explained that he was about to leave for Australia and wanted a snapshot of Lauder Ha' to take with him.

Said Miss Greta: 'Then how would you like Sir Harry in it, too?'

The boy couldn't believe his good luck. There and then Sir Harry rose from his sun-chair, and posed happily with the lad. He went off down the drive, thrilled to bits. Doubtless that photograph of himself and the minstrel star is one of his proudest possessions today somewhere in Australia.

Hundreds of messages of friendship from people in and out of showbusiness, all over the world, heartened the last gallant months of Sir Harry's niece. In 1966, she suffered a stroke soon after returning from a show's opening-night at the Gaiety Theatre in Ayr, in south-west Scotland, and had to be nursed both in hospital and at home for many months. She found it difficult to speak because of the stroke, but she smiled happily as names were read over to her. The world outside had not forgotten the gallant little Scotswoman.

All her life Greta believed in two little words. She used them every week in life, and they spelt out hope and encouragement for hundreds of people, high and low, both in and out of showbusiness. The words were – 'Thank you'.

Whenever a struggling young comedian did a new act on stage or television, and she liked what she saw, she would sit down and write him a short note saying: 'Thank you. I liked your act.'

Whenever a famous star, such as Danny Kaye or Bruce Forsyth, came to Lauder Ha', she wrote to them next day and said: 'Thank you for your visit. It was good of you to come. You made our day.' She never seemed to realise that the trip to Lauder Ha' had, in most instances, made the day for the star.

Whenever she was the guest of a friend, neighbour or stranger, and enjoyed their hospitality, she went home and sent them, promptly, a happy and sincere little 'thank you' note. This was typical of a fine Scotswoman. She had learned the secret from her famous uncle on the many thousands of miles they travelled across America, Australia and other continents.

'Always say thank you to the people who have shown an interest in you' was the maxim Harry Lauder followed and instilled in his niece during all their globe-trotting. 'Ma wee darlin' Greta', as Harry called her, followed that advice to the letter as she herself kept right on to the end of the road.

A Gift from Henry Ford

HARRY LAUDER LIVED a long and happy life. He travelled widely, and met thousands of people of all races and creeds. He had ample opportunities to learn the rules of living, and to amass a wealth of tips for what many would call 'the happy life'.

The great wee Scot was not averse to passing on the tips he learned along the way. He had come up in the hard style himself, and he remembered useful words of advice from his father and his grandfather, and, more particularly, from his mother who had struggled so hard to bring up her family on so little. All the virtues of the hardy, thrifty Scot had been instilled in him over the years.

The Scot of the late nineteenth and the early twentieth century was the kind of man who struck out independently on his own, and made his mark not only south of the Border – in London – but much further afield in Canada, Australia, New Zealand and the United States.

If Harry had not been a successful stage minstrel, he would surely have been a great and good preacher, passing on his practical tips for happy living. He collected these avidly, using his own long years of experience, and he was aye ready, as he said, to share them with friends.

Harry Lauder believed in himself. He set his sights high, and he was always aspiring to bigger things. He kept ambition under control, but he made the most of his constant wish to improve himself.

Love of home was an over-riding factor with him. So was love of a good wife, of children, and of pets. Many of his music-hall stories concerned Scotsmen who got drunk or 'fou', and went rolling home, happy as they came. But this wasn't to suggest that Harry Lauder, once a keen member of the Band of Hope in his schoolboy days, approved of anyone taking too much alcohol.

'Noo, dinna drink ower much!' he would often advise younger men. 'Oh, and dinna smoke too much, either. Aye keep things under control.'

Harry Lauder joked for years about the value of money, and he himself became, through dint of hard work, a very wealthy man. But he never put love of money first. Another of his tips for happy living was this: 'Never abandon love in your search for gold. Gold can wait, but love won't always do as much.'

Often, puffing contentedly at his pipe, he would sit in his favourite armchair at Lauder Ha', and tell friends: 'Naw, naw, laddie. Money is not the key to success. And if you want to prove it, just think o' all the millionaires in Amer-r-rica who have committed suicide!'

He had a shrewd, practical approach to living, and to his work. He knew he had to strut around, often pose as a comical figure in the world's spotlight. Of his work as a comedian, he once told me: 'Ach, laddie, there's no' much use in a man bein' and actin' daft if he's no' tae be weel paid fur it!' How well put!

Sincerity was part of his make-up. He showed a burning honesty in all he did. He was frank, sometimes slightly brusque, but he spoke from the heart. It paid off for the poor laddie from the Scottish coal pits – in large dividends of comfort and happiness.

He was a superstitious man, as many in the theatrical business so often are. My story about his shoe covered with white heather proves that, I think. But he didn't sit there waiting for good fortune to knock on his dressing-room door.

'Dinna count on good luck any more than on bad luck,' he would often tell friends in the profession.

His recipe for living could be summed up: Work hard, but enjoy yourself. It was a recipe that appealed so much to his friends in America, where that maxim is so well and truly adopted even today.

Harry Lauder aimed at success, and made no bones about this being his aim.

'Success is never impossible,' he would say. 'Just you grin and sit up, and reach out a bit further each day – until you get a good hold of it.'

He was a man always ready and willing to take a chance. He didn't believe in hesitating.

'The world is too full of people who preach over-prudence,' he often told his family.

Lauder, who had mixed with go-ahead Scots abroad, believed in the go-ahead spirit. 'In business,' he said, 'enterprise usually earns its reward.' His own enterprise was proof enough. Setbacks and misfortune he encountered often, especially in his early days. But he had a tough tenacity and an ebullient spirit to meet them. And he adopted this procedure to deal with them.

'Sitting doon under hard knocks is the worst thing possible,' he would say. 'Get on wi' the next job in hand. That way, you feel less sorry for yourself.'

His recipe for happiness is not a new one, but it is worth repeating here.

'Keep busy making other people happy,' he would constantly tell other people. 'That . . . that is the secret of *real* contentment.'

But happiness, according to Harry Lauder, must not be made a too obvious goal.

'The quickest way to be happy is to forget all about happiness, and just to work hard at the job in hand,' he said, many a time. 'Keep busy, and you keep happy.'

And, of happiness itself, he would declare: 'Aye, I'm tellin' ye. Happiness is one of the few things in this world that doubles every time you share it with someone else.'

His final dictum, as he sang so often, was to 'keep right on to the end of the road.' He wrote this song after his son's death, knowing it would give him a new aim if he followed it. This message, and the Lauder song, have inspired more people than one would care to count.

All his life he was a simple, practical man. He made a gr-r-rand philosopher, spicing his good advice with happy songs. Harry Lauder knew the real secret of good living.

A busy life, and many years of travelling, left him with little time for the normal hobbies and relaxations and recreations. His career was packed with engagements, and when he eventually retired, he was too old for the sports he might have taken up.

It was in 1909 – he had then completed two fabulously successful American tours – that he decided to splash out on his first car. It was a proud moment when he took delivery of the year's latest model.

It was a 35/40 hp Nagent-Hobson car. He purchased it from Messrs H M Hobson Ltd, aircraft component manufacturers, of Wolverhampton, and Harry, by this time an established variety star, called at their London offices in Vauxhall Bridge Road to complete the transaction.

It was to be the first of a number of handsome cars owned by Lauder, who always had a man to drive him around. One of his last Rolls-Royces, after being sold in Scotland, went in recent years to Toronto, Canada, and is sometimes used there yet in the cause of showbusiness when visiting Scots entertainers drive through the streets in it as a publicity stunt. The surprising thing is that Harry Lauder and his Rolls often get more spotlighting and publicity out of the stunt than do the artistes who are using his car for that purpose.

The vehicle that was shipped out to Toronto from Scotland was a two-tone 1929-vintage grey Rolls-Royce, once a regular sight outside the stage-door of the Empire Theatre in Edinburgh when Harry Lauder starred there. It was shipped to a Canadian in the music business and sold to him for £1,500.

In Lauder's touring days through America, Henry Ford, the automobile magnate, became one of the Scot's staunchest supporters and friends. He used to visit Harry backstage and tell him that few artistes made him laugh more heartily.

'Och, no' tae worry, Henry lad,' Harry would crack back. 'I've laughed mysel' at more Ford motor-car stories than at any other joke in the book!' It was friendly banter between the two men.

Ford got to know Lauder well during many dressing-room chats at the Shubert Theatre in Detroit, and became a personal friend of Harry and Nance. He drove personally to Lauder's hotel and conducted him to his works in the very first Ford sedan to be turned out at his famed Detroit plant.

'So you like this automobile?' said Henry Ford, noticing that Nance Lauder was admiring it to an unusual degree. 'Right, then, I'll ship you one over to Scotland. It will be the first in Britain, and maybe it will help sell it over there.'

Henry Ford was as good as his word. In due course, a trim Ford sedan reached the docks in Liverpool, was transported up to Scotland, and landed outside the Lauder home at Dunoon. What excitement it caused, this American-style car on the country roads of Argyllshire! Harry Lauder was driven in it over Scottish roads for many years.

Lauder's interest in the early motor-cars of this century brought him in touch with other manufacturers in America, including the two Dodge brothers, whose vehicles became famous throughout the USA.

Golf was another of Harry Lauder's spare-time interests – in what spare time he managed to devote to himself, usually in the mornings while on tour. He played at St Andrews (during his tour with Mackenzie Murdoch in 1898) and Southport, and on many, many courses in America, where the US Presidents were his frequent partners. He had many games, too, in Australia and New Zealand during his concert tours there. His favourite golf course, he often said, was the one near his home at Kirn, near Dunoon, on the Clyde. Scenically, this was among the finest in the world, said Lauder, and he had played golf in many lands and against many settings.

Harry's interest in golf stemmed from his own boyhood days as a caddie on the links at Musselburgh. Having been one himself in far less lucrative days, he took a specially close interest in the welfare of those who caddied for him when he became a star, and he often regaled audiences at the 'nineteenth hole' with humorous stories about caddies.

Fishing, however, was Harry Lauder's greatest relaxation, as, indeed, it has been, and still is, for so many whose daily lives are immersed for most of the year in the frantic hurly-burly of show-business. He was in his own 'seventh heaven' whenever he could snatch a day or two to travel north to his favourite stretch of the River Dee, near Banchory, in north-east Scotland. It was on the Dee that Lauder caught his very first salmon as a young man, and he never forgot the thrill of that moment.

Later he was to go fishing all over the world – from New Zealand to California – but he voted the rivers Dee and Don in Scotland the best to be found anywhere for sport. Another favourite spot was Dupplin Loch, where he fished on the estate of his friend Lord Forteviot.

Harry became a most enthusiastic angler, and amassed a quite considerable knowledge of the sport. On one trip to Australia he was taken by some friends to sample the deep-sea fishing off the coast of New South Wales. It was here he landed his first shark, nearly six feet long.

Lauder claimed that New Zealand was the world's greatest paradise for anglers – next to Scotland! He personally fished most of the rivers in South Island, and landed the kind of trout that bring joy to any seasoned angler. He had many happy hours of relaxation with rod and line.

The Lauder Stick

NOBODY HAS EVER discovered exactly how Harry Lauder chanced upon the most unusual, least expected and baffling of all stage props. I refer, of course, to the knobbly walking stick which he featured in his act, and which became, in due course, his long-standing trade mark in theatres and photographs.

If he had lived a little later in this century, many people might have accused him of using it as a 'gimmick'; which would have been most unfair, for Harry Lauder was one entertainer who hadn't the slightest need for such a distinguishing mark. His talent and personal magnetism was more than any one artiste needed to register sufficiently with audiences.

A small and sturdy stick, twisting in little spirals, was something so simple, yet so odd, that only an artiste with a straightforward and simple song act like Lauder could have thought of it. The stick typified the sturdiness of a stalwart wee Scot like Harry. It matched-up alongside his little bow-legs, a physical position which, I need hardly add for those who knew him at home, he always accentuated on the theatre stage, and so set off the image that he wanted to create.

Harry never meant to make these bits of wood the 'gimmick' they became. The crooked stick which he carried and pointed at audiences simply became an intrinsic part of his act. Audiences loved the idea, and fans would vie with each other to find him new walking-sticks.

The Duke of Windsor, when he was Prince of Wales, often

brought back a stick for Lauder from his world tours. He and Harry were good friends. The Prince always called them 'Harry Lauder curly sticks', and was highly amused by them.

When people invited Harry Lauder to official luncheons or dinners, it was easy for them to choose a token of their appreciation of the Scotsman and his work. They simply arranged to make another wee 'knobbly stick' from local wood, and to present it to him as a souvenir of his visit to their town or city, state or province.

Many of the sticks were brought home in this way from overseas tours. Others came from different parts of Britain. One which he proudly treasured was presented to him at a luncheon in Carlisle, in the north-west of England, given in his honour by the directors of Her Majesty's Theatre there in May 1936 by the then Mayor of Carlisle, Mr J R Potts. This stick was then over one hundred years old and had been cut by Mr Potts's great-great-grandfather.

On his own American and Australian tours, Harry was always being presented with crooked sticks. One stick came all the way from Japan. It was taken home to Britain by the then Prince of Wales as a gift. Immediately he saw it, the Prince remarked: 'I must take that home to London for my friend Harry Lauder.'

The sticks – Harry himself preferred to call them his 'twisted sticks' – were greatly suited to accompany his world-famous little dance. This consisted of a curious little twirl or turn which was accentuated by the little sturdy figure and the wiry legs of the star.

As one enthusiastic woman admirer once put it of Lauder, 'Faith, he makes ye laugh just wi' yon swing o' his kilt an' his wee back steps, ye ken!'

Another lady, from Renfrew, in the west of Scotland, went into rhyme to enthuse over this body movement:

Wha wadna gang an' hear the famous Harry Lauder?
Ma grannie heard him sing last nicht, and noo ye canna haud her.
The way he jumped and jouked aboot, juist like a perfect twaddie,
I ne'er in a' ma livin' days saw sic a funny body!

All these comical body actions with legs and feet were helped
to a very great degree by the added effect created by what I like
to dub the Harry Lauder 'knobbly sticks'.

Incidentally, if you are a collector of walking-sticks, you have
the right to dub yourself as a 'rhabdolphilist'. Harry Lauder was
never a lad for the big and unusual words, and he never even
regarded himself as a collector. Amassing the sticks was just one
of the many curious and pleasant side-effects of his globe-trotting
entertaining.

Generous man that he was despite the 'meanness' publicity,
Harry Lauder often gave away one of his curly sticks to people he
liked. After Lauder died, his niece Greta gave some of the sticks
away to close friends.

Before the minstrel reached the end of the road, Danny Kaye,
on a leisurely day-long visit to Lauder Ha', showed such interest
in the wee knobbly sticks that Sir Harry presented him with one.
It was a gesture Danny appreciated to the full. In fact, he was so
proud of that little crooked walking-stick that he seldom let it out
of his sight, had it locked securely away in his hotel suite, and kept
a firm grip on it all the way back to California. Within a few
weeks he was featuring it in his cabaret and television act, and
telling international audiences the story of how he came by it. It
led, naturally, into his impressions of the great Sir Harry Lauder.

When Danny Kaye visited Glasgow in 1949, right at the height
of his variety fame in Britain, one of the first personalities he
sought to meet was Sir Harry Lauder. Their meeting was a direct
result of an approach made by myself as secretary of the Scottish

Critics' Circle. We were anxious to entertain both Sir Harry and Danny to lunch, and a date was suggested; I still have the cable containing Kaye's enthusiastic reply to the idea.

The two stars struck up a friendship, and Danny couldn't listen long enough to Lauder. Or study him sufficiently. He first met him in the Central Hotel, where Danny was staying during his week at the old Glasgow Empire, and later was invited down to see him in his own home at Lauder Ha'.

I met them both during this period, and marvelled at the way two such great entertainers of such diverse temperaments and generations took so readily and warmly to each other.

The Scot and the American got on together quite famously. Harry told Danny stories of his own life and work, and Danny listened, entranced. Then he taught him how to sing *Just A Wee Deoch-an-Doris* ('afore ye gang awa' '), and how to say, in the correct Scots, the phrase 'It's a braw bricht moonlicht nicht the nicht!'

Danny returned in due course to America, and all he could talk about, in his stage act, was that memorable meeting with the wee Scots laird of Lauder Ha'. He recounted stories of their meetings to Americans, and proudly showed off the knobbly stick that Lauder had gifted to him when he left. Then he did impressions of Harry singing typical Lauder songs.

It all went down extremely well with the new generation of Americans, most of whom knew the name Harry Lauder but could only remember him from stories handed down by their parents.

Before long, as was inevitable, the idea of making a film of Sir Harry's great romantic story cropped up. That set the cat among the tartan pigeons! Everybody began to argue the vexed question of who would or could take the part of Harry Lauder.

William Morris, the son of the man who had put Lauder on the road to fame in the States, flew to Glasgow to meet the Lauder family and to talk over plans for the future. He went down to the old Metropole Theatre (once the Scotia, where Harry had played in his very early days), and looked it over. He even hired a professional photographer to take pictures of the theatre, both inside and outside, so that he could have them beside him in America if ever they decided to make a feature colour movie of his career. Alec Frutin, the proprietor of the Metropole, gave him every co-operation.

For a time it looked as if the 'bio-pic' might actually be made. The contenders for the role of Lauder seemed to be legion. Yet the film biography was, at that stage, only an idea, a dream in the eye of many a producer searching for a really good showbusiness story.

In the United States somebody suggested Danny Kaye. It was a topical suggestion, for hadn't Danny only recently returned from visiting Scotland and meeting the great minstrel in person. At this proposal hundreds of Scots saw red! Oh! the impertinence of the idea, they exclaimed. Fancy putting forward an American entertainer to play the part of so noted a Scotsman!

'Don't let it be Danny Kaye!' Hundreds of Scots said that as the arguments were tossed back and forward. They felt this would have been the final insult to a great man. The correspondence columns filled up angrily with letters on the topic. One of the points most frequently made was that Danny Kaye was a fairly tall fellow, and Harry Lauder, after all, was a small man in stature, if big in world renown. Purely on a physical basis such casting would never do, the patriotic Scots argued among themselves.

Just as Scots rise up in arms when it is suggested that a star like Bing Crosby should play Rabbie Burns, the great poet hero of Scotland, so they do likewise when it is proposed that an American like Danny Kaye or Mickey Rooney should take on the role of Harry Lauder.

As this book is being written, there are no fresh plans anywhere to make a film biography of the Scottish minstrel star, although the idea is fairly regularly brought out for an airing. Whether it would be better for a Hollywood company to tackle the story rather than a British one is another moot question. People can argue that one out for months as well.

My own feeling is that a Scot (and Andy Stewart, physically the correct build, must be a 'natural') should portray Harry Lauder if ever a film is made, but that America, where he conquered so many times, should be the country to produce it – using, of course, expert Scottish advice all the time. There are so many locations both across country and in New York that could be used.

It is a natural story for a full-scale film biography, bringing in all the greats of showbusiness over so many years. It is a warm and human story of a poor boy who achieved the heights in fame and fortune, and who lived to walk with kings and queens without losing the common touch.

One day the Harry Lauder story must be told for the cinema screen. Even in AD 2000 the world will be remembering him.

Danny Kaye, of course, was not the only man to imitate Harry Lauder.

Joe Laurie, the distinguished American showbusiness expert and authority on vaudeville, used to say that Harry Lauder from Scotland was 'one of the most imitated men in the world'. He linked him with Charlie Chaplin, Gallagher and Shean, and Jimmy Durante in this connection.

Joe used to joke: 'Say, just try and find me a guy who hasn't tried to sing *She's Ma Daisy* with a Scotch burr!'

Mickey Rooney once donned the kilt and tried to do a Lauder impression. He had the swagger almost perfect, but oh, no, not the accent!

On Lauder's home territory the native-born comedians of Scotland have been, naturally, more perfect at Lauder impersonations. Probably one of the best has been little Alec Finlay, veteran Auld Lang Syne comedian, who impersonated Lauder for so many years. Alec had the same height as Harry, and he could show off those bandy legs and swirl the kilt. More important, he had the delivery of Lauder songs well-nigh perfect.

It was an act of love for Alec Finlay, a lifetime admirer of Lauder. Alec was a boy when Harry Lauder was at the height of his fame. He used to stand outside Glasgow theatres and deliberately wait for him to come out of the stage-door. Then he would accidentally brush against him.

After one such encounter with the Great Scot, Alec took his own coat off (despite the fact that it was raining!), folded it inside out, then dashed home, hung it up, and vowed never to wear it again. He was as good as his word; every day after that, he would touch the sleeve that had been in contact with the great man.

For a time, in his own career, which began in 1928, Finlay was even billed as 'The Pocket Harry Lauder'. Like Lauder, he excelled in character comedy and proved a longtime favourite in pantomime and revue.

In more recent times, Andy Stewart and Larry Marshall, Scots-born entertainers, both did the Harry Lauder songs, and achieved a measure of popularity with them. But when Andy Stewart did a BBC television programme called *Scottish Minstrel*, he was clever enough to let it be known he was not impersonating the great man but merely singing the well-loved Lauder songs.

Harry Lauder kept all his walking-sticks together in the Curio Room which he displayed so proudly to visitors to his home at

Lauder Ha'. After his death, they were taken care of by his niece Greta, and shown off with equal pride to guests at the house. When, in the springtime of 1966, following Greta's death, it was decided to sell off by auction most of the Harry Lauder relics, the wee crooked walking-sticks were in great demand. People travelled from many countries to bid for them. Some two thousand catalogues listing the various relics were distributed round the world, and hundreds of Harry's admirers from the past wrote asking friends and relations to bid for a Lauder stick on their behalf. They wanted them as souvenirs for their homes and dens and bar-rooms.

Hundreds more were at Lauder Ha' in person to try to buy one of the famous curly sticks. Their sentimental and souvenir value was high. After all, Sir Harry had always carried one of these sticks when he sang his great little song *I Love A Lassie*. All of these sticks had journeyed somewhere with the entertainer on his theatrical travels.

They were a proud and yet a rather sad sight, all these silent walking-sticks, as they lay huddled together in a marquee at the auction sale close to the mansion-house that had once known so much life and fun in Harry Lauder's time. Many thought, as I did, that it was a shame to see them being auctioned off to the end of the earth. How much better it would have been if some magnanimous Scot had bought them up and preserved them for all time in a Glasgow or Hamilton museum.

The collection of several dozen curly sticks fetched good prices at the auction. People bid from £8 to £33 for them. The latter bid was made by Mr H W McCurdie, of Seattle, USA, a retired shipbuilder, who made the bid by transatlantic post.

The first ten of the sticks went for £178. Then competition intensified. In slightly over an hour, forty-six of the famed Lauder sticks were sold for a sum that totalled over £800.

This three-day auction sale at Lauder Ha', hit the headlines of the world's newspapers and magazines. Admirers wrote from many lands asking for souvenirs. The requests, with bids, came from South Africa as well as from Canada, Australia, New Zealand, England, Ireland, France – and, most of all, from the USA.

Jimmy Logan, the Scottish theatre star and impresario, bought up many of the relics. One was the original piano on which Harry Lauder had composed his song-hit, *I Love A Lassie*. He paid £100 for it. Logan, wisely, set up a miniature Harry Lauder museum in the ocean-view apartment which he rents in historic Culzean Castle, in Ayrshire, in the south-west of Scotland. Into it he put the Harry Lauder relics to treasure for a lifetime.

But there were many, I know, who felt that Scotland itself, as a nation, should have been prouder than it was of its greatest entertainer. Some move should have been made by, say, the National Trust for Scotland or a similar body to preserve for all time the Harry Lauder mansion in Lanarkshire and the museum of valued curios that went with it.

It could have become a real treasure-house of Lauder memories and song, and a valuable show-place for millions of tourists, particularly American, on trips to Bonnie Scotland. For Harry Lauder automatically ranks with whisky, Robert Burns, haggis and the great Cunard liners whenever the name of Scotland is mentioned in faraway places, particularly the United States of America.

I found myself a lone voice in the wilderness when I wrote an article about the need to conserve Sir Harry's mementoes in his homeland. Many quietly supported me – but nobody took action.

Here are precious relics – song sheets, pipes, old playbills, medals – that surely deserve a place at home in Scotland.

Assembled together, they could form a priceless collection to display to visitors and tourists for all time . . .

Sir Harry Lauder himself knew what Scotland meant. He would have been the last person to want his relics to leave these shores. What use will they be in some theatre enthusiast's collection in a private home in Pittsburgh or Philadelphia?

It isn't too late for Glasgow, as the city that first encouraged and knew Sir Harry's talents, to make a bid for the most precious of these relics. They could be bought by the city and placed in a special Lauder collection in the city's already world-famous Art Galleries. Over the years they could be displayed proudly to thousands of tourists and visitors as part of the theatrical heritage of our land.

Alas, Scotland did nothing to save the Lauder collection. It was spread far and wide to individual buyers in many lands. What a damning apathy and inertia from the land that Lauder made so famous across the seas! If they can preserve the Robert Burns homes and relics, surely they could have done the same for Harry Lauder, knight of the realm, Freeman of great towns and cities!

It was, I fear, more a case of familiarity breeding contempt. Of a prophet being without honour in his own country. The late and famous Scots playwright, James Bridie, had the attitude of too many modern-day Scotsmen summed up to a nicety when he said that too many of them are apt to exclaim: 'Och, Johnnie Dougal! He's nae guid – I kent his faither!'

Those Harry Lauder walking-sticks hanging on the proud wall of a home in Kentucky are an indictment of every present-generation Scotsman.

The Last Act

HARRY LAUDER HAD been seriously ill for some months when he died on a Sunday night at the end of February, in 1950. He was seventy-nine years old. The end, on the 26th February, was not unexpected, although he had joked and laughed with his family on his birthday the previous August. He was in good health and fine spirits then, but suffered a stroke a few weeks later.

I remember well that seventy-ninth birthday on the 4th August 1949. A three-tier birthday cake sat in the centre of the table at Lauder Ha'. The guests were mainly family folk and Sir Harry entertained with a favourite song.

Greta Lauder's mother, Harry's sister-in-law, was there, as she had been at all of Harry's birthdays in the latter years of his life. She always made a dumpling, Scotch-style, for the 4th of August, and, in the good old Scottish fashion, usually put two or three threepenny pieces into it. Sir Harry and the family joked about this, and used to say: 'Maybe we'll be a bit reckless this year, and put sixpences and shillings in it instead.'

In these quiet eventide days, Harry Lauder took life comfortably, as well he might. He had amassed a very considerable fortune from his life's work, and the royalties from his gramophone records and his songs still trickled in steadily as people played his tunes or sang his songs all round the globe.

He used to have breakfast in bed, and sometimes his lunch, too. But he was active for his years, and used to visit all the main

theatrical shows in Glasgow and Edinburgh, where a new generation of kilted comedians were starring. Nothing pleased him more
than to be in the audience when an American star like Dorothy
Lamour or Frank Sinatra or Bob Hope came to town; he felt this
was repaying some of the kindness and good fortune that had
come his way when he himself, a stranger, played in their home
country.

He would regularly attend celebrity concerts in the St Andrew's
Hall in Glasgow when stars like Sophie Tucker were topping the
bill. He was regularly in the audiences, too, at the Empire, Pavilion
and Alhambra theatres in Glasgow, and at the little Gaiety Theatre
in the holiday town of Ayr, where he had a personal link over
many years with the proprietor, Ben Popplewell, and his two
sons, Leslie and Eric. One of his last theatre calls was to the
Metropole in Glasgow to see the well-known Scottish vaudeville
group, the Logan family, in an Irish revue.

Harry joined in the singing of all the good old Irish songs. He
knew what good audience reaction meant to any artiste. I remember watching him singing *The Rose Of Tralee*, and soon the
entire theatre audience were joining in with him.

But the last weeks of his life were sad ones for all who knew
him best. He would occasionally revive to talk with his faithful
niece Greta about his days on the stage, or to hum snatches of his
songs. And, now and then, he would ask for his beloved pipe and
tobacco.

When the end came, the news of his death went winging round
the world. Few Scots were so famous internationally. The
American Press devoted columns to his death, with large photographs of him in the *New York Times* and the *New York Herald-
Tribune*.

The writer in the *New York Times* paid him high tribute.

'So long as the world loves singing, so long will Harry Lauder live,' he wrote.

He was a great comedian – but, more than that, he was a great entertainer, a beloved minstrel; more than that, Sir Harry Lauder was an artiste of superlative finesse, blessed with a combination of wit and voice and personality, and an understanding of the simple thoughts and desires and emotions that make up so much of life.

He was known and loved in four continents.

So, on a cold grey Scottish day in March 1950, the great ones and the not-so-great of the land gathered to pay their final tribute to Sir Harry as he reached the end of a long and notable road. The skies were dark, and there were tears in the eyes of humble folk as they lined the roadways and streets around Hamilton. Blinds were drawn out of respect in most houses.

There were six carriages all filled with flowers, and hundreds of cables came to Lauder Ha' – from dukes and duchesses, earls, viscounts, knights, actors and actresses. The world was remembering with pride a great little man.

The funeral cortège made its way, very slowly, over the five country miles from the Lauder mansion near Strathaven to Cadzow Parish Church in Hamilton, the town where he had worked as a miner and where he first met Nance, his beloved Lady Lauder.

The skies cleared suddenly during the funeral service, and, through the church windows, the sun shone brightly into the handsome Scottish kirk, lighting up the brass-handled oak coffin.

Sir Harry's family and personal friends were there. So were his fellow-comedians from Scotland – Harry Gordon, Dave Willis, Jack Anthony, Jack Radcliffe, Alec Finlay, and Charlie Kemble. The mourners included the Duke of Hamilton and Lord Inverclyde, Sir Alexander King (a lifelong friend) and Sir Patrick Dollan.

The congregation sang *Lead, Kindly Light*, one of Sir Harry's favourite hymns. There was a hush in that quiet old parish church as the minister, the Rev T F Harkness Graham, spoke his tribute to the world star.

'His name,' he said, 'will stand alongside the great names in Scottish literature, if not in the great depths of his poetry, certainly in the desire to put the hallmark of sincerity on our literature.

'He followed in the footsteps of Robert Burns and Sir Walter Scott in choosing the best in Scottish character, in the love of nature and of Highland hills, and in the simplicity of courtship and marriage.'

He called him 'the best ambassador Britain ever had'.

As the coffin of Harry Lauder was carried out for the last time, the church organist slowly struck up the tune he made famous, *Keep Right On To The End Of The Road*.

Winston Churchill and his wife sent a large wreath of lilies, tulips and irises to accompany Harry on his final journey. On the card were written these words: 'In grateful remembrance of a grand life's work. From Winston and Clementine Churchill'. Below the Churchill wreath lay a simple posy of violets – from Margaret Petty, a little girl in Mansfield, Nottinghamshire. She had sent a postal order for half a crown 'to buy flowers for the grave'.

The coffin was gently lowered into the grave in the Bent Cemetery in Hamilton, alongside other members of the Lauder family.

The sun disappeared again behind the grey clouds, a damp Scottish drizzle came on, but more than a thousand folk who had cause to remember Sir Harry personally took time to file slowly past his grave, a final gesture of respect and love from those who knew him best. The wreaths from the great names of the world stretched for thirty yards from the graveside. The people of

Hamilton, Scotland and Britain were still filing past the grave when darkness came down on the little Scottish cemetery and the gates had to be closed.

It rained in Hamilton, Scotland, that March day. It rained, also, on the grave of Sir Harry's beloved Nance up in lonely, lovely Glen Branter, in Argyllshire. It was probably raining, too, on the grave of their son John in that faraway war cemetery at Ovilliers, in France.

Harry Lauder had come to his 'happy abode' after keeping right on to the end of the road. The final act had been played in the wonderful life of a truly Great Scot.

APPENDIX

The Songs of Sir Harry Lauder

Bella McGraw
Bella, The Belle O' Dunoon
Bonnie Hielan' Mary
Bonnie Leezie Lindsay
Bonnie Maggie Tamson
Bonnie Wee Annie
Breakfast In My Bed On Sunday Mornin'
Calligan, Call Again!
Fou The Noo
I Love A Lassie
I'm Looking For A Bonnie Lass To Love Me
Inverary
Is That You, McAllister?
It's A Fine Thing To Sing
It's Nice To Get Up In The Mornin'
It's Nice When You Love A Wee Lassie
I've Loved Her Since She Was A Baby
Just A Wee Deoch-an-Doris
Killiecrankie
My Bonnie Bonnie Jean
O'er The Hill To Ardentinny
Queen Amang The Heather

Roamin' In The Gloamin'
Same As His Father Was Before Him
Saturday Night
She's The Lass For Me
She Is Ma Daisy
She Is My Rosie
Stop Yer Tickling, Jock!
That's The Reason I Noo Wear A Kilt
There Is Somebody Waiting For Me
The End Of The Road
The Saftest O' The Faimily
The Sunshine O' A Bonnie Lass's Smile
The Waggle O' The Kilt
The Wee Hoose 'Mang The Heather
The Wedding O' Lauchie McGraw
The Wedding Of Sandy Macnab
Tobermory
We Parted On The Shore
When I Get Back Again Tae Bonnie Scotland
When I Was Twenty-One

Index

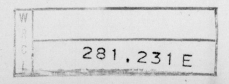